T0208060

"*Thriving in a 24/7 World* is another coaching masterpiece produced by Peter Jensen that helps us frame, manage and maximize the impact of our precious life energy. This informative and easy to read book is full of great tips and advice on how we can turn the tables on our 'perceived' negative stress, grow and, ultimately, perform at our best."

Rick Hansen
Man in Motion and CEO, The Rick Hansen Foundation

"Anyone with the mental and physical energy of a chef should read this book. Dr. Jensen's light & witty style gives a recipe for success!"

Michael Bonacini
Oliver Bonacini Restaurants and MasterChef Canada

"Dr. Peter Jensen has created an easy read with a lot of substance and wonderful life advice. The book provides great insights as to how you, as an individual, can have more energy, create better relationships and achieve Olympic level results in pursuing your goals. It is not a normal theoretical book, but an entertaining novel seen from the eyes of a sports psychologist based on his experience working with diverse groups and individuals. I fully recommend this book!"

Johann Olav Koss
Founder, Right to Play and Four Time Olympic Gold Medalist

"Beautifully written. As you read it you will feel as if you personally are sitting with Peter and listening while he explains, inspires and just generally shares his wisdom about how you can leave behind old habits of being a thermometer, and finally be the thermostat you want to be."

Julian Barling, PhD
Borden Chair of Leadership, Queen's School of Business

"Peter has a great gift to weave important concepts through stories and anecdotes. I have used many in my own career. This is a must read for anyone serious about overcoming adversity, growing team culture and enduring pressure.

I have applied much of his great wisdom to my own life and career. This book does a great job of not only speaking to the topics of resiliency and performance on demand, it gives real life examples and tools to handle them. Pressure is a privilege."

Hayley Wickenheiser
Four Time Olympic Gold Medalist

"In *Thriving in a 24/7 World: An Energizing Tale about Growing through Pressure*, Peter Jensen imparts unforgettable anecdotes and wisdom derived from his vast experience as a coach in both the elite sport and corporate worlds. This book has compelled me to think differently about how I manage my own energy and the value of personal energy management in the performance of my team and my company. Jensen succeeds in engaging the reader by writing in a storytelling style. I devoured the book; it was hard to put down, except to get a good night's sleep!"

Phonse Delaney
President and CEO, FortisAlberta

"For more than three decades, Dr. Peter Jensen has made a long-standing, meaningful and successful contribution to the Canadian

Olympic Team. Serving as the Canadian Olympic Team's Mental Training Coach since the Calgary 1988 Olympic Games, he is now helping athletes prepare for the upcoming Rio 2016 Olympic Games.

In this highly entertaining and evocative book, readers can learn how to separate themselves from the pack by acquiring the unique skills that Peter has taught countless Olympic athletes and corporate leaders alike."

Caroline Assalian
Chief of Sport, Canadian Olympic Team

"It is only the most gifted authors who can use a simple story to convey complex and nuanced messages. With his latest book, Peter Jensen has done just that.

Using the metaphor of a thermostat, combined with the idea that energy management can be a tool we can use to achieve our goals, Peter has cleverly woven a readable, entertaining and insightful story. The concept that we can all use energy to our own personal and organizational advantage, along with practical techniques that can be implemented quickly, makes this a book you're sure to enjoy. In the context of today's demands from a technology and information perspective, this book and its suggestions have never been more relevant to anyone interested in expanding their personal reach and impact."

Shirlee Sharkey
CEO, St. Elizabeth Health Care

"Peter's brilliance once again shines through. Few books truly lead to positive changes in their readers' lives. This one, most certainly, will."

Dave Chilton
AKA The Wealthy Barber

THRIVING
IN A 24-7
WORLD

THRIVING
IN A
24-7

An Energizing
Tale about Growing
through Pressure

WORLD

PETER JENSEN, PhD
with Michelle Kaeser

THRIVING IN A 24-7 WORLD

An Energizing Tale about Growing through Pressure

iUniverse books may be ordered through booksellers or by contacting:

iUniverse
1663 Liberty Drive
Bloomington, IN 47403
www.iuniverse.com
1-800-Authors (1-800-288-4677)

ISBN: 978-1-4917-7233-1 (sc)
ISBN: 978-1-4917-7235-5 (hc)
ISBN: 978-1-4917-7234-8 (e)

Print information available on the last page.

iUniverse rev. date: 10/13/2015

CONTENTS

ACKNOWLEDGEMENTS

Many years ago, I was working with Michael Smith, the decathlete. While we were talking about individual sports, such as track and field, he made the point that in today's world, there is no such thing as an individual sport. He pointed to the fact that he had coaches in each of the events that make up a decathlon. He had a massage therapist, a physiotherapist, several medical doctors, nutritionists and several others on his integrated support team.

It turns out that this need for collaborative effort is also true for those of us who write books. I have had a tremendous support team who assisted me in creating this work. At the outset, my team at Performance Coaching Inc. encouraged me to take on the project and proofread each chapter. Shelley Swallow, Sandra Stark, Peggy Baumgartner and Dane Jensen made up that squad.

One of the most intelligent actions I took was hiring Nikki Baumgartner, a Queen's commerce student, to assist in doing the research for the book. Nikki was incredible. She was an excellent sounding board for content and brought fresh eyes and great enthusiasm to the project. Even after she returned to university to complete her fourth year, she continued to weigh in on each chapter as I completed it.

My neighbour, Jane Harrison, a corporate lawyer at Corus, was kind enough to introduce me to Gord Harris, a veteran of the radio industry, who educated me on open-line radio shows. Gordon was incredibly generous with his time and information when Nikki and I spent an afternoon with him.

Approaching Michelle Kaeser to co-write the book with me was the best decision I could have made. Michelle brought each of the chapters to life. Not only does she have exceptional writing skills, but she also understood the content and made numerous small tweaks, and a few major ones, that dramatically improved the work as a whole. Most of all, she was a pleasure to work with.

My colleagues at Queen's University, Lisa Hendry and Salman Mufti, have always been supportive, and they organized two presentations on the book content in Toronto so that I could road-test it with a business audience.

My final acknowledgement goes to all the wonderful teachers, both formal and informal, whom I have learned from over the years. Some were actual teachers, but most were athletes, coaches and business professionals who, over these many years, have passed on much wisdom to me.

Thank you, one and all!

INTRODUCTION

This book is about becoming a thermostat.

Now, why in the world would you want to become a thermostat? Well, that's best explained by reading what follows, a story about a sports psychologist named Kenneth Coghill and his many adventures with an IT company, a radio show and a world-class basketball team. Still confused? Let me try to explain.

I'll start with the story part. Learning should be fun and easy, and sometimes there's no better way to learn than by reading a story. I learned a great deal about finance from Dave Chilton's book *The Wealthy Barber*. I better understood teams as a result of reading Patrick Lencioni's *The Five Dysfunctions of a Team*. This book, *Thriving in a 24-7 World*, is a story about learning to manage your energy so that you not only perform better but also live a healthier and happier life. Why is energy management the key to these goals? That's a question we'll answer in a non-story format in the last few pages of this brief introduction. Following our energizing tale is a summary of our energy management model and the skills covered in the story. Although the rest of the book is fictional, none of the information is. It's all real and based on considerable research, which, on its own, is boring to read. Transforming all of that research into a fictional story, however, makes the learning a lot more fun—as it should be!

I've based the main character of this book, Kenneth Coghill, on myself. His experiences are similar to my own, except that Kenneth is a licensed psychologist. Central to those experiences is a love for coaching. That's what I am at the heart of things—a coach. Nothing excites me more than helping others get better at whatever they're trying to do. I like to connect with people, see what they're capable of and challenge them to demand more of themselves, and I've been lucky enough to have the opportunity to do that in both the corporate and the elite sports worlds.

My life sits at the crossroads of business and sports. I'm a lover of sports, particularly the Olympic kind. I've attended eight Olympic Games as a member of the Canadian team, and I'm gearing up for a ninth, busily preparing athletes for the summer games in Brazil. I love sport for the sake of sport, but I also love how sports serve as a terrific performance laboratory. I'm constantly taking lessons from sports and applying them to my work in the corporate world, whether as a consultant or as an instructor at the Queen's School of Business.

My diverse interests have pushed my thinking—and research—in many different directions. I've always been a great consumer of a wide variety of information. Even as a child, I had a relentless curiosity that pushed me to read whatever I could get my hands on. This habit persisted into adulthood (and now into what I affectionately call "advanced adulthood"). But the best information, in my opinion, has always come by way of a good old-fashioned story, and if a healthy dose of humour exists in that story, all the better.

As a coach, I use a sense of humour as one of my main tools. Humour reminds us not to take ourselves too seriously. So I've tried to infuse this book with my own strange blend of humour—I've been told that my sense of humour is a particularly eclectic blend. I don't know if that's true, but if it is, then I blame W. C. Fields, the Monty Python boys and wonderful writers, such as Tom Robbins (oh, how I wish I could write just one paragraph like Tommy Rotten) and many others too numerous to mention.

I'm providing this brief background in order to give you an introduction to me and my experience. As you delve further into the book and acquaint yourself with dear old Kenneth, the story will reflect and expand on this information. As I said, he's a close stand-in for me—except he has a different wife. Of course, there's nothing wrong with my wife; she's an incredible woman whom I love dearly. However, the book afforded me a chance—without losing 50 percent of my assets—to try out a new relationship. But the truth is, despite my best efforts, my book wife ended up being much like my current wife. What can I say? Old habits die hard.

Let's get back to this business about the thermostat. I was looking for a metaphor that would best capture the idea of energy management. Eventually, I settled on the idea of a thermostat—but that wasn't my first idea. My first idea came by way of a basketball coach down in Texas.

I was in Houston a while back, doing a corporate presentation on coaching skills. One of the senior leaders, Larry, came up to me at the end of the presentation to comment on how much he'd enjoyed it. One of the things I'd spoken about was the importance of using pressure or stress in a developmental way as a tactic for creating healthy high performance. This approach is something we use in sports with our elite athletes. We make sure that pressure and the handling of it are seen as part and parcel of growth toward becoming an excellent performer.

Larry told me he was mentoring a young basketball player. The young man constantly talked about how much pressure he was under with all the major and minor pressures, challenges and stressors in his day-to-day life. Larry brought out two basketballs. He bounced one of the balls several times and passed it over to the young man.

"How's this ball?" he asked.

The young man bounced it a few times and said, "It's fine."

Then Larry punctured the second ball—an older ball—with a penknife. He passed this flat, unresponsive ball to the young man and asked, "How about this one?"

The young man looked puzzled and wasn't sure what to say.

"You see—it's the pressure that gives things their bounce," Larry said.

What a terrific story and piece of coaching! I thought I could take Larry's metaphor even further. Like a basketball, we all have an optimal psi (pounds per square inch), a level of pressure at which we bounce best. With too little pressure, we're flat. With too much, we're overinvigorated—like an overinflated basketball, we bounce out of control.

I loved Larry's story so much that I was tempted to use the basketball as a chief way of talking about energy management. But there is a problem with this metaphor: although it makes clear the point that pressure is necessary for energy and growth, it can't account for our ability to improve our handling of high-pressure situations. It can't explain how we become more resilient in the face of ever-greater pressure. The basketball has an ideal pressure that allows it to bounce perfectly, but that pressure is constant regardless of the situation.

So I needed another metaphor.

A colleague, Dr. Harvey Silver, was the first to introduce me to the concept of the thermostat. The idea here is simple. You want to be a thermostat, not a thermometer. A thermostat sets the temperature. A sophisticated thermostat will constantly tweak the temperature to ensure it's at the ideal level for any particular situation. When sleeping, for example, many people prefer a lower, cooler temperature than they do when they're up and about during the day. The thermostat makes these adjustments. It doesn't matter what the outdoor temperature is; inside, the thermostat creates ideal conditions.

A thermometer, on the other hand, simply rises and falls to reflect the environment. It's reactionary. It has no control over things.

There's a lot of skill involved in managing and moderating energy levels. In a heated, high-pressure environment, people without thermostatic skills will see their energy levels rise to match the environment. They'll get heated, amped up and even agitated. These people are like thermometers. Similarly, when the energy in an environment is low, when it's cold, thermometer-type individuals will find themselves feeling flat. Conversely, thermostat-type individuals can choose to increase their energy, bringing enthusiasm and vitality into a cool, disheartening environment.

In my role as a mental training coach, I work with athletes who have learned to get to the optimal energy levels for their specific performances. Sometimes, especially in repetitive practice situations, when workflows are high and relentless, athletes need to energize in order to fully engage and practice at their best. At other times—in game-day situations, for example—they need to lower their arousal levels and return to a better, more-productive energy.

Your skill level and the complexity of the task you're doing will determine your ideal energy level. You can perform simple, well-learned skills with much-higher energy levels than complex tasks, especially if those tasks are new to you. As you get better and become more skilled, what was complicated becomes simpler and requires less attention. Therefore, the required energy level changes. We'll cover this idea in greater detail later.

This book concerns itself with the psychological aspects of energy management. Are there other aspects? Yes. Proper and adequate fuel is key. What you eat and when you eat are important considerations for any efficient energy manager. Even the best cars can't run on bad gas. Poor nutrition wreaks havoc on your whole system. Excessive amounts of caffeine, for example, can cause huge energy swings that are difficult to control. Energy management techniques won't be of optimal use if your body is constantly revving up or slowing down as a result of what you've put into your fuel tank. There's plenty to talk about in terms of nutrition, but here's a brief summary: eat food, not too much, mostly vegetables.

Physical fitness is also crucial to energy management. None of the Olympic athletes I work with have normal physical-fitness levels. Of course, Olympic Games aren't exactly normal situations. They are extreme situations and require extreme physical fitness. But even for us normal folk, a reasonable level of physical fitness is important for good energy management. A healthy body is more resilient, bounces back more quickly from adversity and setbacks, handles greater workloads and avoids fatigue and energy depletion.

Although nutrition and fitness are important for our optimal daily functioning, they're not the focus of this book. There is much information on these two areas elsewhere. In their excellent work *The Power of Full Engagement*, Tony Schwartz and James Lohr cover this territory well. In this book, as I mentioned, we'll primarily be looking at the psychological component of energy management. I say "primarily" because we'll talk about rest and recovery, which, although physical in nature, are of paramount importance to the psychological side of things.

To most people, the words *energy management* trigger associations to energy crises, such as electrical blackouts or brownouts, or the price of gas and oil. But when we talk about energy management here, we're talking about you and your own personal energy. We want you to learn how to make maximum use of all of your energy resources. This means not having an internal brownout during an important presentation or when you're at home with your family. It means not depleting your energy with needless worrying and self-doubt. Energy management is all about having the energy to engage in your life when it matters most.

A few years after we founded Performance Coaching Inc., my wife, Sandra Stark; business manager Shelley Swallow; and I were sitting around, trying to capture in a few words what we were all about. We eventually came up with this: we want to help people stand tall, lighten their loads and have more fun. I hope this small book will be another step in that direction.

Now you can choose to move straight ahead to chapter 1 and jump right into the story, or you can read the next section, a summary of some of the pertinent facts justifying the assertion that managing energy, rather than time, is the answer to a better life. The story is energizing and interesting; what follows is less so. Personally, I'd move on. But hey, this is your book, so you get to do what you want.

THE CASE FOR ENERGY MANAGEMENT

We live in a world where the sheer volume of demands we face as professionals, parents and students has grown exponentially, yet the amount of hours in a day has stayed constant. Failing to identify this constant, many people mistakenly turn to time-management strategies in the hopes of keeping up with their growing list of to-dos. But time is finite, and it's outside of our control. Even when we think we're using our time wisely, time often has control over us. The pressure of time has us forfeiting well-needed nights of sleep. The urgency of time creates waves of anxiety in us. The limits of time force us into thinking we don't have enough of it to spend with the ones we love most in this world. Time is the problem; it is not the solution.

Energy management, on the other hand, is within our control. It's about striking a balance between moments of high performance and periods of renewal. Getting enough rest and recovery, leveraging our stressors and enjoying the presence of our loved ones are positive actions connected to energy management. These actions serve to increase our level of productivity at a greater rate than the couple of extra hours we spend working in a worn-out, disengaged state.

Consider, for a moment, the following situation, which you are probably all too familiar with. You've run out of time during the day, so you decide to pull an all-nighter to punch out the last few pages of a report. What are the consequences? In the best-case scenario, you've jeopardized your entire next day of work. Thanks to Dr. Charles Czeisler, professor at Harvard Medical School known as the Sleep Doctor, we now understand the exact damage that sleep deprivation causes to our bodies and minds. His research shows that a person's reaction time decreases threefold after staying up all night—that's basically the difference between being sober and drunk. And that's not all. A lack of sleep will yield a drop in your testosterone, which you need to fuel your muscles and which impacts your ability to make decisions. Ultimately, your body requires testosterone for optimal performance, and a week of sleeping for just five hours a night or less can lower your testosterone level to that of an 11-year-old boy. Isn't it funny how we praise employees for working at the expense of a good night's rest, but we'd never dare applaud employees who show up to work drunk?

Remember—a poor performance the next day is the best-case scenario. In the worst case, lack of sleep is linked to a whole string of health issues, including high blood pressure, heart disease, diabetes, weight gain, depression and even death. From 1982 to

1988, Dr. Daniel Kripke and colleagues conducted a study on 1.1 million people in order to see if sleeping patterns were associated with mortality rates, and in fact, they are. Kripke and his colleagues found that the individuals who clocked in seven hours of sleep per night had the greatest survival rate. Those who slept fewer than four hours a night had a mortality rate that was, on average, two and a half times higher. Sleep is one of the greatest ways our bodies can seek recovery. It is interesting to note that Kripke and his colleagues also found that those who slept more than 10 hours a night had one and a half times the mortality rate. It appears ideal recovery is between six and a half and eight hours a night.

The more we focus on time, the more we begin to realize a fundamental reality: we don't have enough of it. This realization often brings on a big wave of stress, which can consume our thoughts. But stress is only a problem because we've made it a problem. Stress doesn't have to be the monster that sabotages our performance or acts as a drain on our health. In fact, when leveraged correctly, stress can create mental resilience and increase clarity. It's your body's way of preparing itself for the challenges ahead. Therefore, good energy management is not about avoiding stress altogether but, rather, about leveraging your body's stress reactions in order to better your performance.

Stress can even do more than just benefit your performance—it can also enhance immunity. A more-recent study, conducted at the University of Wisconsin School of Medicine and Public Health, tracked 30,000 adult participants from the United States for a period of eight years.[1] At the start of the study, subjects were asked two questions:[2]

1. How much stress have you experienced in the last year?
2. Do you believe that stress is harmful for your health?[3]

---

[1] A. Keller, K. Litzelman, L. E. Wisk, T. Maddox, E. R. Cheng, P. D. Creswell, and W. P. Witt, "Does the Perception That Stress Affects Health Matter? The Association with Health and Mortality," *Health Psychology*, September 2012.
[2] Danielle Elliot, "The Doctor Who Coaches Athletes on Sleep," *Atlantic*, April 23, 2014.
[3] Daniel Kripke, "Sleep Deprivation: The Great American Myth," *LiveScience*, March 23, 2006, Web.

After the completion of those eight years, the researchers consulted public death records. Those who reported experiencing a lot of stress in the previous year *and* fostered the belief that stress was harmful had a 43 percent higher chance of dying. Those who experienced as much stress in the previous year as the first group yet did not believe stress was harmful for their health had the lowest chance of dying—even lower than those who reported having little stress whatsoever. After extrapolating and applying the results of this study to the entire US population; researchers estimated that more than 20,000 Americans die each year from the belief that stress is harmful for them. Kelly McGonigal,[4] a Stanford University health psychologist, explains that if this extrapolation is accurate, "stress beliefs" chart the list of most-common causes of death in the United States at number fifteen. That means these stress beliefs are "killing more people than skin cancer, HIV/AIDs, and homicide." There's no question that learning how to make stress work for you is a critical part of optimal energy management.

Enough already! You get the picture. Now let's get to our story.

[4] Kelly McGonigal, *How to Make Stress Your Friend*, TED Talk, 2013.

CHAPTER 1

THE RADIO SHOW

In this first chapter, we meet our energy management guru KC in his car on his way to do a drive-home radio show with Bill, the show's host. His appearance even lands him a corporate gig!

Kenneth Coghill is 68 years old. He has a PhD in sport psychology. Those are the basic facts. But as is the case with most facts, they don't tell you much about the man himself. The facts don't tell you how KC—as his friends call him—arrived at his current employable state. When individuals, particularly sport psychology graduate students, ask Kenneth what they need to do to get to where he is now, there's no clear formula he can give them. The path he's taken is too windy, unpredictable and organic to use as a template.

Luck and good fortune have played an important role in his life. They have to play a role in order for one to grow up in a northern mining town and end up going to eight Olympic Games, working with more than 70 Olympic medalists, teaching 20 to 25 days a year at a leading business school and making a living by giving speeches on coaching and mental fitness. That's a bare-bones description of Kenneth's professional life. His personal life is an equally meandering tale that will emerge in our story. Let's join that story.

It's four-thirty in the afternoon, and already, rush-hour traffic has taken hold of the city. Kenneth Coghill drums his fingers on the steering wheel as he slowly makes his way toward the radio station. He's scheduled to do a quick guest spot on the five o'clock show as part of the promotion for his latest book on energy management. The radio show is a great opportunity to kick up some publicity for the book—or it would be if he ever gets to the station.

"Why did I agree to do this thing on a busy Tuesday right after a long weekend? This time slot is a nightmare!" KC says to himself, feeling his irritation amplify with each minute he's stuck in this bumper-to-bumper traffic.

KC flicks on his radio. In half an hour, his voice is supposed to be crackling through the speakers, but right now, he hears the sympathetic voice of a traffic reporter who hates being the bearer of bad news.

"It's not looking good for rush-hour commuters," the reporter says. "Delays heading both east and west. And generally slow moving around the city. Good luck out there, folks. Buckle up for a long drive home."

KC doesn't wait to hear any more. He switches the radio off and takes a few deep breaths to try to settle his agitation. "Traffic reports only help if you want to become even more irritated than you already are," he tells himself.

Looking at the road ahead, he sees that he's somehow landed behind a courier van, its four-way flashers blinking as it inches along at a pace so slow it seems to defy reason. KC hasn't been keeping track, but it feels as if this is the fifth courier van he's managed to get behind this afternoon. He swerves the car a little to the left and then a little to the right, hoping to earn a better view of what's ahead. More traffic—that's all he sees.

Somewhere in the pages of his book, he's written about this type of experience—a commute can be irritating in a different way every day. There's a lot of advice in that book that would help him right now. It's too bad the frustration clouding his mind is making it impossible to access any of it. This is not a great mental state to be in for a discussion on how to most effectively manage energy. KC tries to remember his own advice, and he tries to steady his breathing in order to lower his arousal level, but the *honk-honk-honk* of a car to his left almost immediately interrupts these efforts to calm himself.

"What? Who's honking?" he shouts to no one in particular, an exclamation of pure irritation.

But when he turns to find the source of the honking, instead of a road-raging lunatic with a trigger-happy honking hand, he sees a kindly driver on his left, waving him into her lane with a gentle smile on her face.

It's a small gesture—nothing but good manners, really. However, the act of kindness is enough to erase KC's irritation and bring him back to his senses. He shakes his head at himself. He ought to know better. Getting irritated about things he can't change is a waste of energy. But even an expert on energy management isn't immune to the stresses of downtown traffic.

"A little wake-up call from the universe," KC says with a chuckle.

And just in time too. Right up ahead, he sees the sign for the radio station.

The studio is a beehive of activity. The five o'clock show draws the biggest audience for the station, capitalizing on the throngs of evening commuters who have nothing better to do than fiddle with their radio dials. Amid the bustle in the studio, KC finally spots Bill, the host of the *Drive Home Show*.

"Heya, Kenneth," Bill calls out with a big smile. If KC had to describe Bill with just one word, that word would be *friendly*.

Bill weaves around a few hustling people as he crosses a hallway to get to KC.

"Busy today, huh?" KC says.

"Always is," says Bill.

Bill leads them through the winding corridors toward the recording booth. They enter the room just in time to catch a promo for KC's upcoming segment: "Have you wondered how to correct the course of your life? How to develop better parenting skills? How to perform at an Olympic-gold-medal level for years on end? Well, good news. Coming up at the top of the hour, we've got energy management expert Kenneth Coghill joining us in the studio to help you sort out these issues."

"Wow, I'm supposed to do all that in twelve minutes? I must be good," KC jokes.

The studio is a small, modern and technologically up-to-date space. A U-shaped table dominates the room. There's a chair at the head of the table, the host's position, and two chairs along both sides of the *U*. Each of these spots is equipped with a microphone on a boom that can be used whenever needed. Across from the host's chair sits the board operator, who gives KC a friendly nod, but he doesn't have time to do more than that, because he's absorbed by the several computer screens and the soundboard in front of him. This guy handles all of the technical aspects of the show and keeps everything running on time.

Bill pulls out a chair for KC and then takes his own seat at the head of the table. He slips on his headphones, and a few minutes later, they're on air.

After a quick intro of KC and his background, Bill asks his first question. "So, Kenneth, the book is called *Thermostat 24-7*. Let's start with that. Why that title?"

KC chose the title because he thought it concisely summed up his strategy for energy management. "It's a reference to a metaphor I like to use," KC says. "About thinking of yourself as a thermostat as opposed to a thermometer."

"Can you explain that?"

"Sure. A thermometer measures the temperature outside. That's how it operates. It rises and falls based on what's happening around it. But a thermostat sets the temperature of the environment. So be your own thermostat. Set your own energy level."

"I like that. It's easy to get your head around," Bill says.

From there, they delve into some of the ideas in KC's book. One of the first things KC talks about is the difference between energy management and time management. "After all," he says, "you can have all the time in the world, but if you don't have the energy, you won't make it through a single item on the to-do list."

"That's an interesting distinction," Bill says. "I never thought of things that way."

Bill is a seasoned host and interviewer; he and KC quickly fall into an easy on-air banter, and the session flies by. In fact, when the board operator signals them to wrap it up, KC is caught by surprise—he's barely scratched the surface of his book's content.

"Well, our switchboards are lighting up with callers here," Bill says. "But it looks like we've only got time for one or two."

It's a relief to KC to hear that his segment has generated a solid response from listeners. He's confident about his ideas, but he knows they can't work unless people are open to changing the way they operate. A crucial part of his teaching—of any teaching, really—is that the students, whoever they are, must be ready for and receptive to a new way of thinking. KC is reminded of Cynthia Scott, who works in organizational development in California. She was once asked, given the demands on her time, how she chooses her clients. Her response stuck with him. Among other criteria, she always wanted to know if the would-be clients, the CEOs, had had either a heart attack or a grandchild in the last few years, because either of those events tends to open people up to change.

Of course, KC has no way of knowing if the *Drive Home Show*'s listeners have had grandchildren or heart attacks in recent years, but the flood of calls lighting up the board at least suggests an interest in what he's saying. Maybe a long, exhausting day at the office topped off with an almost-as-long drive home reminds energy-depleted listeners that there might be more-effective ways to navigate life. Maybe it reminds them to consider change.

Bill hits a button to broadcast one of the callers. "Hi, Marie from Leaside," he says. "You're on the air."

"Oh, hi," says a soft voice. "What you're saying, Kenneth, really hits home for me."

"I'm glad to hear that, Marie," says KC.

Marie goes on to describe how the constant stresses and pressures of life make her underperform at her job. She's expending most of her energy thinking about the piling pressures she's under. It exhausts her. KC immediately recognizes the choker's profile, a common theme in sports. He's spent 30 years working with Olympic athletes, helping them overcome the sometimes-debilitating pressure of high-profile competition. Choking at the Olympics is one thing, but Marie is describing something else. KC sees in her someone who has been stuck in the choker's profile for a decade or more.

The second caller Bill puts through expresses similar concerns. KC wishes he had more time to dig in deep with these callers, to find specific and personalized ways to help them work their way out of the choker's profile. But before he has time to say more than a few words, Bill is already wrapping up the segment. KC's 12 minutes are up.

After Bill sends the show to a commercial break, he takes a look at the computer screens that track listener response, and he gives KC an encouraging smile. "Wow, we're getting a lot of response here—calls, tweets, e-mails. Great segment."

Although flattered by the attention, KC is disappointed that he didn't have more time to get into some of the particulars, the specific techniques of learning to manage energy and be one's own thermostat.

On the drive home, KC reflects on the day with mixed feelings. By all accounts, it was a successful interview, but still, he wishes he could have done a little more.

Several days later, just as KC returns home from a long morning run, the insistent ringing of his phone greets him. When he answers, he hears the station manager, Roberto Molina, on the line, calling with a proposal: "We got some great feedback from your appearance on the show, Kenneth. We think there's a lot more to mine there. And so we're wondering—would you be interested in joining Bill more regularly? We were thinking of having you do a series of one-hour guest spots. We'd like to do it as a monthly special—one appearance a month for the next five months."

"Wow, uh. Hmm. That's an unexpected offer."

KC thinks about the proposal briefly. He had a great time at the studio, and he loves the idea of doing some more in-depth work, but it would be quite a commitment. Furthermore, KC's used to working with people face-to-face; he likes being able to read their expressions and gauge their reactions. Working with people over the radio would be a different challenge. As a coach, though, he likes new challenges and ways of helping people excel. This format definitely fits the bill. Besides, KC was never one to shy away from new ground. It's the runner in him—"New ground, new energy" is the runner's refrain.

Roberto explains—a bit sheepishly—that there wouldn't be any money in these appearances. "But of course, it would be great exposure for your book."

KC can't argue with that, and he can't say no to a challenge. He's decided. "All right, Roberto. I'm in."

"Great—just great. We'll get in contact in a few days to work out the details. But glad to have you with us."

"Okay, great. Talk to you soon."

KC is about to hang up the phone, when he hears Roberto's voice pick up again: "Oh, oh, wait!"

"Hm?" KC asks.

"One of our major sponsors, Optimal IT, called in after the show. They were looking to get in contact with you."

"Oh yeah? What about?"

"They've been having some personnel trouble over there. To be honest, it sounded to me like they're in a bit of a crisis. They're looking for help—any help. They'd like to bring you in for a consultation. I'll send along their information if you're interested."

KC knows he should take a look at his schedule first to make sure he has time to take on a new client. But he's not always that prudent. He's an optimist, and one of the symptoms of that affliction is the tendency to take on a dozen projects at once, fuelled by the belief that things will somehow work out. "Sure, sure, please do," KC said. Then he adds, "This would be a paying gig after all, right?"

"I guess that's true," Roberto says with a defensive laugh. "But we might also look at it as just another example of the power of marketing on radio."

CHAPTER 2

OPTIMAL IT

In this chapter, we discover that KC is a meditator who gets easily distracted. We also meet Karen at Optimal IT, a company having some construction and energy management issues.

Sitting cross-legged on his bedroom floor, KC breathes in and out in a focused rhythm. This is how he begins every day—with a half-hour meditation. It's a habit he picked up a decade ago after attending a 10-day total-silence meditation program at Vipassana Meditation Center in Massachusetts. Given KC's extroversion and the fact that he speaks for a living and just likes to talk, his decision to undertake a silent meditation program astounded his closest friends. No one could imagine him sitting quietly for 10 days. He'd never even managed to sit quietly for 10 minutes around a dinner table!

When he returned from the meditation program, he described it to his wife, Wanda, as one of the noisiest things he'd ever done. "When you try to train your mind to focus on a single thing, it's amazing how agitated and noisy it gets," he told her. "The mind constantly wants something new to focus on."

"I'm still just amazed you were able to be quiet for that long. It seems like a miracle!"

"I was only outwardly quietly. Inside, everything was loud."

"Still, I'd take it!" his wife joked.

KC laughed and then continued his reflection on the nature of the mind. "It's funny how, here in Western society, we all think we are our minds," he said. "But let me tell you—anyone who tries to meditate for even five minutes will realize that the mind and the man are very different things."

"Or the mind and the woman," Wanda adds.

"Right, of course."

KC thought then about how insistently the mind always wandered off. One of his favourite quotes came from the Chinese philosopher Lao-tzu, who once said that the mind is like an untrained horse—it runs everywhere.

As he meditates this morning, KC recalls this nugget of truth from Lao-tzu. As much as he tries to stay focused on his breathing, his mind has other plans. It keeps drifting toward a phone conversation he had yesterday with the HR director at Optimal IT, a woman named Karen.

Now, it's not unusual for women to pop up in KC's meditation space. When the mind wants to be distracted and entertained, attractive images often become the focal point of the mind's cravings. But a yearning for attractive images isn't what sets his mind wandering today. This morning, the cause of his drifting attention is another favourite distractor in meditation practice: the desire to analyze.

During his brief conversation with Karen, she invited him to come in today to discuss the many problems plaguing Optimal IT. She didn't give him much in the way of details, so KC's mind has been busy imagining a dozen different possible scenarios in play at Optimal IT, and already, he's mentally preparing his approach to this new client. When he realizes his mind has slipped away from his breathing, he does his best to redirect his attention to the point where the air enters and leaves his nostrils. Without judgment, he brings his concentration back to his breath.

His meditation teacher, S. N. Goenka, referred to this non-judgmental approach as being equonomous. In meditation practice, you try not to wrestle with all of the thoughts that crop up. Instead, you patiently direct your mind to what you've decided to focus on. For KC, this focus is his breath, his nostrils. *In and out. In and out. In and out.*

Soon the gong of a meditation bell sounds from his iPhone timer, telling him his 30 minutes are up. It's time to get on with the day.

Optimal IT sits on the edge of an industrial park. It's a large, single-story, pleasantly rambling sort of structure on a beautiful wooded lot. A few months earlier, while driving by this area, KC noticed the structure. At the time, the peacefulness of the setting had struck him. He saw picnic tables under the heavy trees, where he imagined people eating lunch or gathering for outdoor meetings. It seemed idyllic.

But today, *peaceful* and *idyllic* are the last adjectives that jump to mind. The place is a hotbed of construction. He sees diggers and trucks everywhere, construction workers milling about and a parking lot that's cramped and crowded. All of the commotion makes it hard to remember the calm the place could inspire.

KC notices construction indoors too: torn-up walls along one side of the corridor, emptied rooms. In the reception area, Karen, who seems to have been eagerly awaiting his arrival, greets KC. She's a tall woman with an athletic build. Her short blonde hair nicely frames her warm and intelligent face. She has the look of a woman who likes to get things done. KC likes her right away.

"Thanks for coming, Kenneth," Karen says, offering a solid handshake. "And on such short notice. Can't tell you how much we appreciate it."

"Sure thing. Happy to be here."

"Sorry about all this construction," Karen says as she steers him down a hallway away from the worst of the noise. "I booked us a meeting room just down here, where I hope we'll at least be able to hear each other over the jackhammering. It's the quietest room we've got. But still, there's really no escaping the noise."

"This place has a whole different feel than I remembered," KC remarks.

"Oh, have you been here before then?"

"Just as a passerby. I drove by a few months back. But I remember thinking how serene the place seemed. To be honest, I'm a bit shocked at the level of construction you've got going on here."

"If you think you're shocked, imagine how our employees feel! They're all used to operating in a calm environment, a wooded oasis."

They arrive at a small room at the end of the corridor, and Karen ushers him inside. "Actually, the construction might be the perfect place for us to start our discussion," she says.

"The construction is your problem?"

"Not exactly. But all this racket and the frantic energy you see are pretty indicative of what's going on inside the company as well. We've been undergoing some big changes. Frankly, we're in chaos."

Through an open window in the room, KC hears the shouting of a construction worker, followed by a thundering crash. Looking outside, he sees a cluster of workers gathered around a pile of lumber that has unexpectedly spilled out of the back of a truck and fallen into a trench running along the side of the building. "Sure seems like chaos," KC says.

Karen joins him at the window. She must have become used to such mishaps, because she lets out one quick sigh and then closes the window and turns to KC with her enthusiastic expression back in place. She gestures for him to take a seat at the long table in the centre of the room, around which are a half dozen mismatched chairs, more evidence of the internal disorder in this place. "Maybe it's best if I tell you a little about the history of our company—how we got to be where we are now."

"I think that's a good way to start," KC says.

As KC sinks into a wobbly chair, Karen begins to explain the history of Optimal IT.

The company was formed by four MIT grads 35 years ago. For 30 of those years, they provided IT support for small- and medium-sized companies, and in so doing, they were able to maintain a gradual and manageable rate of growth. The company policy was to be choosy about the clients they took on, selecting clients in professional fields—particularly health and medicine—who were also growing slowly and with whom they could keep apace. But over the last five years, things changed. Optimal IT doubled in size and now employs more than 400 people. In just the last six months, the changes have been even more dramatic. The company has gone through an IPO. Two of the original partners have left. The office space, obviously, has been undergoing a complete overhaul. All of this rapid growth has brought with it pressure to expand the business in new ways, chiefly by taking on larger clients.

To do this, Optimal IT recently purchased Zanzibar, a former competitor who has more experience working with larger clients. Although similar in size, Zanzibar has a history and culture different from Optimal IT's. Two brothers started Zanzibar right out of high school—renegades in the field. They took on anything and everything that came their way, so their company developed a different, looser culture. Despite a plan for integration, the culture clash has proven to be more of an issue than the companies anticipated. It's had a clear and negative effect on employees. People are frustrated with the inefficiently functioning teams, the lack of progress and the long hours. Things have gotten so strained that one of Optimal IT's most-valuable new employees, Dominic—a main reason for the Zanzibar acquisition in the first place—has been threatening to quit if matters don't improve.

"What we need, Kenneth, is to get Optimal IT running as smoothly as possible. We need a common vision. We need to reorganize. And we need to do it fast, because people here are fried. And there's no relief in sight."

KC blows out a huge sigh as he takes in the scope of the disorder here. "Wow," he says. "Forgive the pun, but things sure aren't optimal here at Optimal IT."

Karen responds with an easy smile. "I always forgive puns. I have a weakness for them."

"Then I think we'll get along just fine."

It's a pleasure for KC to see that even amid all the stress and chaos, Karen is able to retain a sense of humour. He's spent less than an hour with her, but he's already impressed by her attitude. "Let me ask you a question," he says.

"Anything."

"What did you hear on that radio show that made you think I might be able to help?"

"Well, actually, I'd been looking for people who might be an asset to us for a while now, and your name came up a few times. So when I heard you on the radio show, I thought it was synchronicity telling me to reach out to you."

KC mulls over the information Karen has presented, and he can feel various ideas and strategic approaches start to float around in his head. This is a big project. A lot of areas require attention. But if he can help guide Optimal IT through this period of change and get them back on a successful trajectory, it will be a great achievement. He's still in midcontemplation when Karen pipes in again.

"Look, I know dramatic changes are needed here. But I want to find ways to support the amazing people we have working here—the ones who have been with us for years and the ones who are just joining us. This may sound corny, but I think as an organization, we have a responsibility to eliminate major stressors if we can or, if we can't, to at least strengthen our people and help them work through the stress with greater ease."

KC beams a smile at her. Her words don't strike him as corny at all. They're sincere and optimistic. KC is a sucker for both of those qualities. "You have no idea how refreshing it is for me to hear that," he says. "Where did you develop that kind of thinking?"

"I was a volleyball player in university—varsity. But there were so many ups and downs—injuries, setbacks and all that stuff. It got to be that I couldn't cope. I lost my love of the game. I thought I'd quit. But then, near the end of my first year, we started working with a sports psychologist. Kim was her name. She taught us how to turn pressure into development, how to act when we were able to make a difference and how to let go when weren't able to. Those skills have served me well over the years."

Here's a woman who's speaking my language! It's not often that

KC meets someone who's on his wavelength. The idea of having Karen as an ally bumps up his excitement for the project. Always expressive with his excitement, KC slaps a hand on the table. "Karen, it's going to be an absolute pleasure working with you. I don't remember ever meeting a client who so clearly understood the philosophy of what I do—and I haven't even really told you what I do yet!"

"Good point. What is it exactly that you would recommend here?" she asks. "What would you do?"

KC explains that initially, most people associate the term *energy management* with environmental concerns. However, when KC uses the term, he refers to something more personal. "Personal energy is perhaps our most-valuable resource," he says.

"You mentioned that on the radio show. It really intrigued me. I was especially struck by your thermostat metaphor. I've never really looked at things through energy management glasses. Well, hang on now; that's not true. I guess I did when I was an athlete."

"I'm not surprised. Athletes are constantly expending huge amounts of energy, so it's crucial for them to be aware of how they're using their energy. And of how they're going to regain it, fill up the tank."

"That's the rest-and-recovery element, isn't it?"

"It is. And elite athletes aren't just aware of how essential regaining energy is. They're also acutely aware of how often their perspectives, their way of looking at things, can influence their energy resources."

"I recognize that. I was introduced to that idea—the sport psychology angle—as an athlete. In terms of energy, I was heading in a downward spiral. And it was just because of the way I was thinking about my game."

"That's why time management isn't always the answer. A lot of people think if they manage their time well, they'll perform better. But the amount of time we have is finite. We don't have any control over that. But we do have control over our energy. It's really about learning to strike a balance between moments of high performance and periods of rest and renewal. It's also about learning how to minimize the drain on our energy."

"So what would this look like as a program here at Optimal IT?"

KC describes his ideal. He'd like to conduct a series of workshops with each of the departments at Optimal IT. The workshops would be spaced two to three weeks apart, and each workshop would feature strategies that employees could apply to the workplace between sessions. He's found that several interventions over a period of one to two months is most effective in helping skills stick. The goal is to get people using the skills he teaches them so that they can become more productive, less stressed and more satisfied with their work.

When KC finishes detailing some of his ideas, he pauses to gauge Karen's reaction. She looks pensive, but it's a bit difficult to read the nuances of her expression, and he worries he's overwhelmed her. "I know that's a lot of information, Karen, but I wanted you to see all of it. What do you think? Any questions come to mind right away?"

"Nope. I'm on board. But the real concern is that we'll need to sell the idea to upper management. I think the best way to do that is by starting with one small group and demonstrating that your approach can have an impact."

"Sounds good to me. So where should we start?"

"Well, if you're up to the challenge, I'd say let's jump right in with Dominic and his team. They're working with a new large client called Metronome. This is a big deal for us. It's important that all goes well here. But if we pull things off with Dom's team and with the Metronome situation, we'll have no trouble selling the senior leaders on the whole idea of energy management."

KC hesitates. His instinct is to start with a smaller, more obviously manageable situation, as they'd have a greater likelihood of success. From there, they could build some momentum for his program. On the other hand, if Dominic is front and centre in the eyes of senior management, it would be a coup to effect positive change with him and his team. But it will be no easy task.

"What's wrong?" Karen asks. "You look scared. Have I scared you?"

"It's just that we'll be taking on a major challenge here."

"Come on," says Karen with a playful glint in her eye. "Are you a man or a mouse?"

"Squeak," KC replies.

Karen lets out a hearty laugh. She is a good-natured sort. "Remember what Helen Keller said: 'The timid are caught as quickly as the bold,'" she says. "So we might as well go for it!"

CHAPTER 3

SHOW PREPPING

In this chapter, KC is enlightened by watching children play and comes up with an energy management model for his radio shows.

With the new gig at Optimal IT, the upcoming monthly radio shows and his regular (packed) schedule of coaching and speaking engagements, KC starts to feel the weight of his workload. This kind of sudden realization is not uncommon for optimists. One of the reasons they often end up in energy management crises is because they dramatically underestimate how much time things will take. It's always easy for optimists to see where to start with a new project, to identify the current level of performance, and by their nature, it's also easy for optimists to imagine a rosy ending for any project. It's the middle—all the work, attention to detail, and unexpected and inevitable problems that present themselves—that's murky to the optimistic mindset.

The monthly radio show turns out to be a more-time-consuming project than KC thought. With the first show just around the corner, he's slammed with a string of meetings at the station. Hosting a radio show requires a certain amount of technical know-how, and the show's producers try to guide KC through an accelerated learning process.

"This screen tracks listener feedback," one of the producers explains, pointing to a computer screen in front of the host's chair in the studio. "It identifies callers by name and gives you a little blurb of information about them and what they want to talk about. So you can select who you want to put on air. And this switchboard lets you put the caller through."

KC looks at the equipment in front of him. He tries to absorb everything he's being told, but the information is coming rapidly, and he's not sure he'll have it all down by next week, when the first show is set to start.

Sensing KC's confusion, the producer adds, "Of course, you'll have Bill with you. So you don't need to remember everything. But it's good if you at least have some sense of what's going on."

"It looks like I could operate an international space-shuttle mission with all this equipment here," KC says.

The producer chuckles knowingly. "It seems like a lot—I know. But you'll get used to it."

KC wonders if this is true. Like many people his age, he's used to being unconsciously competent. He's done so many things for so long that they no longer demand any real thought or attention. For the last 25 years, he's delivered close to 200 presentations a year. He knows the content of his speeches by heart, so he's able to speak without getting nervous and to be competent without having to think about it. But figuring out all of the ins and outs of hosting a radio show will require more conscious effort than he's used to. The truth is, it's daunting.

When the producers finish showing KC the technical side of things, Roberto, the station manager, addresses a bigger-picture issue: the layout of the five shows.

"We need you to think about how exactly you'd like to organize the monthly shows," he says. "A clear idea of the topics you want to cover, how you want to break it up. You have any thoughts on that?"

"Well. Hmm. Not yet," KC says.

"Give it some thought," Roberto says, letting an expression of concern show on his face. "We'll meet again early next week and try to hammer out the details."

KC leaves the radio station after the meeting and feels small waves of anxiety begin to ripple through his chest. The small waves soon turn into tidal waves of terror. Has he gotten himself in over his head here? It wouldn't be the first time. While he reflects on this burgeoning anxiety, he remembers Brent Sutter, an NHL coach who suggested that his players benefited from getting afraid early on during preparations for big events, such as the Stanley Cup playoffs. Sutter wasn't promoting fear. He was encouraging advanced preparation. Fear and anxiety are often aspects of that preparation. KC tries to embrace his own anxiety by remembering that it's part of the preparation process.

Over the next few days, he spends all of his spare time preparing for the show—trying to think of how best to structure the five monthly instalments and determining what he most wants to talk about. It's difficult because there's so much to choose from. Dozens of topics connected to energy management get him fired up: nutrition, exercise, spirituality, sleep and recovery—the list goes on and on. Of course, there's no way he can offer an in-depth look at all of these areas. He'll have to narrow his focus and offer digestible chunks of information to his listeners. KC recalls one of his favourite expressions from a friend of his, decathlon coach Andy Higgins: "Focusing on everything is focusing on nothing."

KC most wants to focus on the psychological side of energy management. The physical dimension deserves its own fair share of attention, but he wants his shows to tackle the psychological. He wants to take a look at what's going on inside. Now he just needs to find an interesting way to do it.

On his way into the meeting at the station the following week, KC decides to walk rather than drive. It's a beautiful day, and he jumps at the chance to breathe in some fresh air and soak up some sunshine. He's noticed over the years that people tend to have a lot more energy when they take the time to do things outside. He's developed several (unproven) theories about why this is so. Topping that list is the following reason: the soul loves beauty. Nature is full of beauty, and beauty is eternal.

Wasn't it Garry Zukav who suggested that the soul had one foot in time and one foot in eternity? he wonders to himself as his path leads him through a quiet park.

KC lets his mind wander a little, hoping it will eventually wander toward some kind of inspiration about how to organize his radio shows. Although he's been agonizing over the matter for days, he still hasn't come up with a solid approach. With his meeting just half an hour away, he's battling the dread of impending doom. With every second that passes, it becomes more likely that he'll show up at this meeting and have nothing to suggest. Bubkes. Zilch.

Feeling like a dead man walking, KC remembers a great quote from English writer Samuel Johnson: "When a man is to be hanged in the morning, it focuses his mind wonderfully."

KC laughs at the morbidity of this statement. In 2010, he was diagnosed with throat cancer, and true enough, it focused his mind wonderfully. He went through a horrible yet successful treatment program involving 35 radiation treatments and a bout of chemotherapy. During this period, he described his life as being not dissimilar to a dog's. When he was tired, he immediately lay down and got some rest. He didn't wait or use the excuse "I just need to get one more thing done." When he noticed he was tired, he lay down. It was simple.

That experience was instrumental in the development of his attitude toward energy management. Even before his diagnosis, KC knew he was burning the candle at both ends. He'd read enough research to know that wasn't good for him. But like most people, it took a giant wake-up call for him to adjust his behaviour.

"It's interesting how reluctant we are to change our habits," KC says to himself as he reflects on that time in his life. "Even when we know better. Even when we have enough information to point us in a different direction."

But he knows that sometimes it takes more than information to effect change. It takes a lived experience. In KC's case, he was able to respond to the wake-up call of his illness with a complete change in his behaviour. Now he pays keen attention to his energy levels. Whether in between meetings downtown or before a major presentation, he often ducks down to his car in an underground parking lot, puts the seat back, turns on the sound-machine app on his iPhone, sets the alarm for 20 minutes and takes a quick nap. He's learned to charge his batteries.

From up ahead, KC hears the happy shrieking of young children busy at play. *Talk about fully charged batteries!* KC thinks as he watches two of the children dash from one end of a grassy field to another with great bursts of energy.

He pauses to watch them. Watching children is like seeing exceptional energy management in action. They play with an energy level that older people often comment on longingly. How many times has he heard one of his friends, while watching children at play, say, "I wish I had that kind of energy," or "I don't know where he finds all that stamina"?

But if we want that kind of energy, why don't we do what they do? KC muses, studying them.

The children play hard and then suddenly stop and sit down to rest and recover. A short while later, they're back, fully engaged. When they do this, they're completely focused on their play. They aren't multitasking; they aren't wasting energy worrying about whether they're playing properly or not or whether those watching think they're doing it right or not. They aren't thinking about what they have to do next. They exist in the moment. "Be here now," an old Buddhist saying, is on display right here in front of him.

That's when KC has a realization. Maybe it's because of the sun, the park, the children or his wandering mind, or maybe it's a combination of all of these things, but suddenly, the inspiration KC has been looking for strikes. It comes to him all at once as a complete package: the approach he wants to take for the radio shows. There will be details to flush out, of course, but it's clear to him that there are four key ideas he wants to offer his listeners.

The first is all about clarity; he wants to make it clear to his listeners why energy management is important. If his listeners don't understand the why, they won't be interested in the how.

The second is about regaining energy once it's been depleted. This involves the concept of engaging fully in a task, as the children did, for a short burst of time; taking a short break by doing something different, something energizing; and then getting back on task.

The third point is about adjusting energy levels, both upward and downward, depending on the situation. Before big events, most folks need to adjust their energy levels downward. People most frequently err, as KC has seen countless times in the world of sports, when arousal levels are too high before big events. On the other hand, in day-to-day training with athletes and in the corporate environment, there are times when the opposite is called for, when people need to pump up their energy levels. He wants to address both of these cases—lowering one's energy level when it's too high and raising it when it's too low.

The fourth and final point he wants to focus on is the need for people to minimize the drain on their energy resources. People waste energy all of the time in all kinds of ways. In our homes, for example, we waste energy by leaving lights on, not sealing doors and windows properly and doing a dozen other careless things. Similarly, in our bodies, we deplete energy by worrying, doubting, overanalyzing and getting caught up in the limbo of decision making. We waste energy trying to be perfect, which always gets in the way of excelling. The fixation on perfection is pervasive in our society—and problematic. Sure, it's a great quality in a heart surgeon, but it's less great and less necessary when raking leaves off the front lawn or preparing a preliminary proposal that will be torn apart and reconfigured anyway. Sometimes it's imperfect to do something perfectly.

As he considers this final thought, he glances at his watch and realizes his meeting is in just five minutes, and he's still a block from the station. He resists the temptation to rush, opting instead to walk at his regular pace. There is no point in depleting his mental and physical energy with a last-minute hustle and sprint. It's better to arrive intact energy management–wise; he wants to have healthy stores of energy so that he can focus on the details of the meeting—especially now that he has something to present.

CHAPTER 4

 # BEGINNINGS AT OPTIMAL

In this chapter, we learn about the skill of reframing, the thermostat and high-arousal Henri.

It's a crisp, sunny fall day when KC drives up to the Optimal IT building. The construction seems less chaotic than it did the last few times he was here. It looks as if things have progressed toward the finishing stages. However, from work KC's done on his own house and on his summer cottage, he's aware that the finishing stages of renovations often take much longer than the actual building and construction stage. The small things take forever. But in the end, they make the biggest difference.

Once again, Karen meets KC in the reception area and ushers him down to the now-familiar room at the end of the corridor. Over the last few weeks, he's had several meetings with her, both in person and over the phone. With each meeting, he's more validated in his initial impressions of her. She's a trooper, confident and determined but also realistic—and trustworthy. KC knows she'll go to bat for what needs to be done; she won't bail at the first sign of resistance.

"I'm eager for you to meet Dominic today," she says.

Having decided to start their program with Dominic and his

team, they've scheduled a meeting with him today so that KC can get a better sense of the issues he and his team are struggling with.

"Can't wait to meet him myself," KC says.

"Unfortunately, he's been held up with some crisis in his department. But he's assured me he'll be by in half an hour. To be honest, I'm glad for the delay—it gives me a chance to raise a concern I'm having."

"Oh yeah? What's that?"

As they settle into the mismatched chairs around the table, Karen says, "Given the workload Dominic and his team are battling, they're already jammed for time. So I have a feeling our intervention might seem like just another thing we're piling on their plates. Somehow, we need to introduce the idea of energy management to them in a way that helps them see it as a long-term time-saver."

"And a stress reducer," adds KC.

"Right. But how do we get them to see that?"

KC thinks about the concern for a moment. It's not uncommon for people to be reluctant to take the time to address underlying issues that are causing trouble. In sports, he sees it all of the time, especially in team sports. Often, the relationships among players are tense and strained, but everyone's uncomfortable about digging into that trouble. "We might start with a reframing exercise. I've used this with teams when individuals are afraid to confront others on key issues."

"Sounds good. How does it work?"

KC explains that in his reframing exercise, he first asks everyone to tell him what fears or concerns he or she has about addressing the issue at hand—his or her fears about engaging in a confrontation. The individuals on the team come up with a list, which usually includes the possibility of damaging relationships, throwing the team off course and disturbing the status quo.

Then he asks them to make a list of what might happen if they don't confront the issue and fail to address it altogether. The individuals usually provide pretty much the same list. If the problems are the same whether or not they confront them, he explains, they might as well go ahead with the confrontation and at least give it a shot.

"I think you're onto something here," says Karen. "Let me see if I've got this. What you're saying is, we ask Dominic's team what will happen if they don't take the time to discuss their current situation, and the consequences of that situation remaining fixed. Then we ask them what will happen if they sacrifice some of their time to actually deal with the situation. In both cases, they'll be afraid of falling even further behind in their work. But in answering the second question, maybe they'll begin to see that that option at least offers the possibility of change, an upside. And that might give them enough energy to try to tackle the problems!"

This summary is exactly what KC is thinking. As usual in conversations with Karen, he's amazed at how in sync they seem to be. She's quick to grasp his ideas and even expand on them. "You're reading my mind," he says. "Only we're going to phrase the questions in emotional terms. How will it *feel* if they never confront the current situation? How will it *feel* if things are exactly the same three months down the road or three years down the road? Feelings and emotions are the fast track to the brain. If you want to get people to change, you've got to talk about emotions."

"My goodness!" Karen exclaims, rising a little out of her seat. "This is so in line with a book I read a few years back. It's called *Switch*, by Dan and Chip Heath. Have you read it?"

Now it's KC's turn to be excited. His hands shake as they always do when he gets going on topics that thoroughly interest him. "I have. And I loved it. I particularly love the metaphor they use. It's about the rider—"

"The rider, the elephant and the path," Karen finishes for him.

Delighting in this common ground, KC and Karen trade stories about their favourite parts of the book. They discuss how they might incorporate some of the lessons from the book into their own challenges here at Optimal IT. In their book, the Heath brothers present a simple, usable metaphor—that of a man riding an elephant along a path. The path represents a clear sense of direction, the rider represents logic and the elephant represents emotions. The Heath brothers point out that we spend most of our time talking to the rider. But what we should be doing is talking to the elephant—emotions and feelings—if we want to get things moving.

For many years, in his presentations, KC has talked about the role that emotion and imagination play in growth. Logic doesn't change human behaviour. If it did, who would smoke? Who wouldn't exercise? Who wouldn't eat properly? It takes an appeal to the emotions to find sufficient motivation to make a change.

The reframing exercise KC is suggesting offers this kind of appeal. It allows people to consider their feelings. In particular, it allows them to imagine the positive feelings they'll experience in a future where they confront and resolve their problems and end up working reasonable hours in an upbeat, even fun, environment.

"I love the idea of targeting emotions," Karen says. "It reminds me of another book I'm reading at the moment, *The Heart of Change*. The authors—John Kotter and Dan Cohen—observed that in most successful change efforts, the sequence of change isn't analyze, think and then change. It's see, feel and change. It's all about the importance of emotions."

"Oh yeah, that's another solid book," KC agrees.

"I think this reframing exercise is the perfect way to start. I can't wait to suggest it to Dominic. I think he'll be excited." As Karen mentions Dominic's name, she glances at her watch. "Look at that—he should be here any minute now."

KC can't believe how quickly the half hour blew by. But then again, he's noticed that time has a tendency to zoom along whenever he gets to discuss some of his favourite books.

"Tell me a little bit about Dominic," KC says while they wait. "What's he like?"

"Well, he's an exceptionally popular manager," she says. After quickly glossing over Dominic's management style, she offers up a history of his career. Dominic started out with Zanzibar years ago, when it first formed. Now he manages a group of creative programmers—five employees from the original Optimal IT and six from the newly acquired Zanzibar. Karen is just starting to elaborate on the difficulties Dominic has faced in trying to merge the two cultures, when in walks the man himself.

"Knock, knock," Dominic says with a few quick taps at the doorframe. He's a small guy—short, with a slight build. Apart from this, KC immediately notices two things about him: his bright eyes and his fidgety behaviour. He seems edgy and anxious—like a cat in a roomful of rocking chairs.

KC pops out of his chair, walks forward, puts out his hand and says, "Speak of the devil. You must be Dominic. I'm Kenneth Coghill. And I'm very much looking forward to working with you."

"Oh, oh yes," stammers Dominic. "I'm sorry, but I'm really not sure what you mean when you say you'll be working with me."

Karen quickly jumps in. "Kenneth is the consultant I spoke to you about at the end of the meeting last week, Dominic."

Dominic's bright eyes narrow slightly as he tries to recall the conversation in question, and his features twist into a sort of alarmed confusion. The name Kenneth Coghill doesn't seem to ring any bells. "Hmm."

Karen continues. "I know you're juggling a million things right now, so let me refresh your memory. I asked Kenneth to come here today so that you can hear some of his ideas about how to help us out—ideas about how to help you and your team through this difficult transition period."

Dominic lets out a big sigh and relaxes with relief. "Oh, thank goodness," he says, looking straight at KC now. "For a minute there, I thought you were some new programmer HR was bringing into my group. Okay, okay, I do remember our conversation, Karen. Sorry about that. I'm a bit under the gun just now. I've got so many things on the go. I guess it's easy to forget a few of them."

With a sympathetic laugh, Karen waves Dominic into the room and pulls out a chair for him. "I bet the last thing you want is another programmer to integrate into your merry band."

"We're not such a merry band at the moment, I'm afraid," says Dominic, lowering himself into his chair. Even seated, he doesn't look comfortable.

"That's as good a place as any to start," Karen says. "I wanted you to fill Kenneth in on your group. Talk to him a bit about the integration of the two staffs. I've briefed him on the organization as a whole, but I haven't talked specifically about your department."

"Where do I start?" Dominic says with a tone of exasperation. "I suppose I should start with the general integration. And then I'll finish with Henri."

"Henri?" KC asks. It's the first time he's heard the name.

"Oh boy, yeah. Henri. The integration would be hard enough without him. But with him and all of his negativity, well, it's at least twice as difficult. I just wish he wasn't such a brilliant programmer."

Dominic picks out a pen from a pen cup on the table. He passes the pen through his fingers, fiddling with it anxiously.

"What about the rest of the team?" KC asks. "Tell me how things are going."

Dominic talks at length about the various challenges involved in bringing together 11 people—12, including him—from two different cultural backgrounds. "It seems they all feel threatened in one way or another. The five I've worked with for years are wondering what their place is on the team now that we've added six people. The pecking order had been clear for some time, and they all knew what they were good at. They work really well together, and they trust each other. Adding six people has dropped a bomb of uncertainty on them.

"Now, as for the six new people—the original Optimal IT folks—they're trying to adjust to a different culture and trying to figure out where they fit in. Trust is an issue with them, too. I'm sure we could work this all out if it wasn't for Henri. He's, well, difficult. To put it mildly."

"Let's leave Henri out of this for the moment," says KC.

"Just for the moment? How about forever?" jokes Dominic.

"Well," says Karen, adopting a more-earnest tone, "maybe that's a solution we ought to consider."

But Dominic is quick to shut that idea down. "No, no. When I think about our workloads and the Metronome deadline, we really need all hands on deck. And Henri is the best programmer we've got. No, we need Henri on board. Besides, I'm sure in a week or two, he'll settle down and become a team player. Maybe he's just having a rough time with all the adjustments. I need to make more of an effort with him."

"I hope you're right, Dom," says Karen. "I certainly like your optimism. Just keep in mind that if his behaviour does continue, you and I can always discuss other options."

"Thanks, but it won't be necessary."

"Let's move away from Henri," says KC. "Let's look at your group as a whole. Tell me what an average day is like."

Dominic takes a deep breath as he readies himself to articulate the stresses of everyday life at the moment. "First off, there's the sheer volume of work to be done right now, especially with the Metronome project. Layered on top of that is all the transition stuff. For some, that means learning an entirely new encryption process. For others—actually, almost everyone—that means working with new teammates and getting to know their capabilities. Then there's another layer of demands from departments within the company that need IT help for their people in the wake of the amalgamation. Bottom line is, people are coming in early, staying late and working weekends, and they don't feel like they're really accomplishing anything. And this is maybe the biggest problem: they see no end in sight."

"So how's the team feeling now? What's been the impact on them personally?" asks KC.

"Well, there's the overall fatigue. No one feels like their efforts are fully appreciated. Then there's a lack of hope and enthusiasm. It's like the air has just gone out of them. Only a few months ago, there was humour, vitality and a real sense of camaraderie on my team. Now I can't even remember the last time I heard someone laugh or joke around or even offer up a bit of banter. Unless you count sarcasm. There's been a dramatic rise in sarcasm. But not a lot of fun." Dominic stops fiddling with his pen. He looks at Karen and then at KC and says, "You know, when I lay it all out like this, it's a pretty sad state of affairs."

KC can hardly disagree. But he knows things don't have to stay like this if the team is willing to confront their problems.

For the next half hour, the three of them discuss ideas about how to best stage the energy management intervention. They settle on organizing a half-day workshop the following week.

"I hope this works, Kenneth," Dominic says as he stands up, eager to get back to work. "We need all the help we can get."

Eight days later, KC pulls into the parking lot of a small hotel several blocks from Optimal IT. He and Karen both decided it was important to do the workshop off-site. Both are fans of the Italian psychiatrist Roberto Assagioli, who talks about the need for people to be able to *disidentify*, or step back from themselves and observe things from the position of a neutral witness. In a perfect world, KC and Karen would have chosen an off-site retreat setting, something far removed from the office environment. But Dominic knew that his staff would be anxious to get back to the office and back to work after the workshop, so he suggested this hotel because it's close by. It was a good compromise.

KC and Karen are already in the small conference room when the first of the participants start to arrive. Karen greets everyone with a friendly handshake and personalized hello.

"Hi, Margaret," she says. "Thanks for coming, John. Good to see you, Tracy."

During this load-in process, KC notices that the original Optimal IT programmers are the first to arrive, some by themselves and some in pairs. In contrast, the former Zanzibar employees arrive as a group, as though they're trying to find strength and safety in numbers.

The participants, Dominic included, split up into groups of four around three round tables. Each table is equipped with markers and a flip chart. Understandably, a sense of uncertainty permeates the room. Nobody's sure what to expect from this meeting. A minute or two before the scheduled start time, only one chair remains unoccupied; one person is missing: Henri.

As Karen stands to offer her introductory remarks, Henri slouches into the room with an unenthused expression and slowly makes his way to the free seat. His arrival is noticeably disruptive, his tread is heavy, his jacket rustles loudly and the chair squeaks as he drops himself into it. Karen waits for him to get settled and then begins.

"Thanks for coming. I want to start by explaining why this training session has been scheduled. I want you to know that upper management understands the tremendous pressure you guys are under. And it's clear to them, and to HR, that something has to be done to help you out."

The spirit of helpfulness and understanding in her voice has an effect on the group. KC notices everyone visibly relax in his or her seat and feels the tension in the room start to diffuse.

"So now let me quickly introduce Kenneth," Karen says.

While KC listens to her enumerate his qualifications, he thinks her use of the word *quickly* was less than accurate. She talks about his work in the world of sports, she mentions his work teaching at a top university's business school, and finally, she elaborates on energy management work he's done at companies similar to Optimal IT. KC would have preferred a briefer introduction—he'd like to get right into the work at hand. However, he understands her strategy in laying out his credentials like this. Even among the skeptics, such an introduction establishes him as something of an expert.

As her introduction winds down, KC knows she'll call him up any second. A tingle of nerves passes through him, from the top of his head down to his toes. But the minute he notices this nervousness, he gains confidence. Over his years of presenting, he's learned that nerves and stress of this kind have a strengthening effect. They add to his performance, engage him and get him into the game. He always tells the athletes he works with that pressure is a privilege—it means you're being given a chance.

"And with that, let's welcome Kenneth," Karen finishes, and she gestures for him to take the floor.

KC, energized and ready to go, thanks Karen for the introduction and then dives right into his reframing exercise. "I'd like to kick things off with a little group task."

He likes to open many of his workshops with an activity. Rather than simply lecturing to a group, he likes for the participants to actively engage in the process and the learning. A pet expression of his is "Learning resides in the learner, not the teacher." By getting his audience to answer questions and participate in exercises, he allows them to arrive at key understandings on their own.

"At your tables, work together to come up with a list of the challenges you're experiencing in the workplace. You can use the flip charts to write out your lists."

The participants seem game. Within a minute, he hears them busily discussing their personal and collective challenges. A quick scan of the flip charts shows him that the lists are growing in length. As some groups near the bottom of their first sheet of chart paper, KC notices that the mood in the room has darkened considerably. Forcing them to consider all of their difficulties is having a dreary, disheartening effect. But this is good, as it means they're digging into emotional territory.

When the sounds of discussion start to taper off, KC tries to push things a little further. Gesturing at the charts, he says, "Great. Looks like we're rich in problems. Now I'd like you to look over your lists and discuss how it really *feels* to be facing all this stuff. And then discuss what it might feel like three months from now if things haven't changed at all."

As soon as they get to work on this step, the mood goes from bad to worse. A heaviness descends over the tables, and they all seem to slouch farther down in their seats, their heads drooping forward. It's clear they're having emotional responses to this bleak, projected future.

KC's got them right where he wants them.

"Now let's discuss another alternative," he says. "I'd like you to talk about how you might feel three months from now if all these issues are resolved."

Watching the participants discuss this brighter option for the future, he notices the energy in the room pick up. People sit up in their chairs, their eyes open a little wider and a few smiles make appearances. KC even hears a ripple of laughter sound out from one of the tables, as though someone's just cracked a clever joke. Again, the participants are having emotional responses to the exercise. But this time, the response is positive and uplifting.

"All right then. Let's talk about what needs to happen to get there," says KC. The exercise has had the intended effect. The group is alert and focused now. Everyone recognizes the need for change, and this recognition opens them up to new ideas and approaches—it makes them receptive to the workshop.

"There's no doubt that your current workloads are unsustainable and unreasonable. The organization will do what it can to help lighten those loads. But during this workshop, we're going to look at how to make the absolute best use of your energy. I want to look at four main areas of energy management. The first is something we've actually already covered: it's about acknowledging the need for a change. I think we can all agree that a change is needed. And all change requires adaptive energy. In light of the fact that energy is critical, the next area we're going to cover is how to restore your depleted resources. One of the biggest challenges here might be overriding your natural tendencies to push yourselves. For example, we're actually going to ask you to take more-frequent breaks and get more rest. We want to discourage you from working longer or harder."

"Sounds good to me," says John, an extroverted guy sitting at the front.

"Almost too good to be true," chimes in a female voice from farther back. Some skeptical looks from around the room echo her sentiment.

KC is used to this skepticism. People are conditioned to think that working longer, harder hours yields better results. This belief is a fallacy he's encountered time and again. "One of the many things I've learned from working with elite athletes is that it's not just their training and work ethic that makes them better. It's also their ability to stick to rest-and-recovery programs. The best car in the world doesn't run well without gas. And neither do we."

Some of the skeptical expressions begin to ease as the group reflects on the analogy.

"This brings me to the third area: how to set your energy to the desired level. That means how to energize, both individually and as a group, when you're flat and unmotivated and how to lower your arousal level when your energy is too high. Think of yourselves as thermostats, not thermometers. Don't let the environment control your energy level. Set your energy levels, and make the environment adjust."

Just as KC is about to move along to the fourth area of energy management that he wants to discuss, a woman at the table closest to him interrupts with a question.

"Just a minute, just a minute. Too high?" says Jillian, one of the former Zanzibar programmers. "I don't think I understand that. How can energy be too high?"

This is another question KC gets a lot. Most people think energy management is about finding more energy. However, it's just as much about moderating arousal levels, or setting the thermostat. "Ever been in a situation where you were really agitated or upset? Maybe someone gets under your skin during a meeting, and ten minutes later, when you're back at your desk, you spend all kinds of energy thinking of everything you should have said."

"Sure. Just the other day, I thought Henri agreed with an approach I suggested. I thought that because he said so when we met early in the morning. And yet at our afternoon meeting, he tore into me like I was some idiot." Her voice becomes increasing agitated as she recalls the episode. "I was so irritated that I couldn't even respond during that meeting. I clammed up. But later, at my desk, after I'd calmed down some, I drafted an e-mail saying every little thing I wished I'd told him during that meeting. Never sent it, of course. But it felt good to get it out."

"That's a perfect example, Jillian. In the world of sports, we've got a word for that kind of clamming up: *choking*."

"Whoa, hey, I didn't know she was so upset," says Henri defensively, interrupting. "The whole context of the problem we were working on had changed in my mind from when I talked to her in the morning. I just wanted to save us all some time and get on with solving the problem. Time is of the essence, Jillian. We didn't have time for you to go on and on the way you do sometimes."

Henri's negative attitude catches KC off guard. In barely a minute, the guy has managed to stomp out all of the positive energy in the room. Suddenly, KC has a much better sense of what Dominic was talking about with respect to Henri. But before he can respond, Karen jumps in.

"Let's not get sidetracked by the team dynamics just yet. We'll do some work on that area in the future. Kenneth, you said there were four areas we'd be working with. You've mentioned three. What's the fourth?"

It's clear that Henri is able to exert a dramatic influence on the group. If KC's energy management plan is going to stand any shot of success, he knows he'll have to address the Henri situation. But for now, he agrees with Karen's decision to soldier on. Sensing the collapsed energy in the room, he decides to get things back on track with a revitalizing summary of the progress they've already made. Then he'll tackle the fourth and final area.

"Let's take stock of where we're at so far," he says, pumping some enthusiasm into his voice in an effort to amp up the energy in the room. "It's clear that you're unhappy and want things to change. You've generated some pretty long lists of problems. The current situation is no good. It's emotionally and physically draining. It's generating feelings of hopelessness. It's just not tenable. Agreed?"

Murmurs of assent pass through the room. He sees a small sea of heads nodding in agreement.

"On the other hand, when you imagine this whole situation being resolved in just three months, your emotions are completely different. You're excited! Motivated! Ready for something new! Is that fair?"

This time, the murmurs are a little louder and more confident. The nodding heads are livelier.

"Okay, I've already mentioned the importance of acknowledging the need for change, and I've mentioned how critical rest and recovery are. We've talked a little about setting and controlling arousal levels. Now, the fourth area I want to look at is about minimizing the drain on our energy. This involves the way we think about things, especially things outside our control. Often, we apply all kinds of effort to things, when no amount of effort will change them. It's what I call 'ceaseless striving.'"

This idea of minimizing the drain seems to strike a chord in Karen. She says, "Correct me if I'm wrong, Kenneth, but this fourth area is huge, isn't it? It would include things like worry, doubt and concern. All that stuff doesn't have much positive benefit, but it depletes our energies. So minimizing the drain includes thinking about our perspective and how we talk to ourselves."

"Oh, absolutely," says KC. "The way we think about our problems has such a great effect on us. And a physical effect, too. The minute I start to imagine some of the things my mind is saying to me, my whole physiology starts to change. So yes, the perspective we hold has a huge impact on our energy levels and, ultimately, on our performance, happiness and sense of satisfaction."

KC scans the group to gauge their attention levels. He's managed to inject a little energy back into the room, but he's also just delivered a lot of information all at once. He decides to implement one of the key features of any good energy management plan: it's time for a break.

"We'll go into all of this a lot more later. But for now, let's take a quick break, stretch our legs and have a snack."

As the groups break up a bit, some of the participants wander around the room, stretching lightly. Others cluster together to discuss the workshop so far. KC heads over to the break table in the hall, from which he grabs a bottle of water. Karen and Dominic join him.

"Nice recovery after Henri's little outburst. Talk about sucking the energy out of a room," Karen says.

"Try sitting at a table with him," Dom adds. "Boy, does he ever make things difficult. Either he gets really quiet and sullen and refuses to engage, or else he comments on how stupid all of this is, what a waste of time it is. It's exhausting."

"Well, I'm glad you're sitting with him," Karen says. "I know it's not easy, but maybe you can help keep things on track at that table."

"I'll do my best. But he has a real talent for wearing everyone down."

Fifteen minutes later, KC is back in command of the room. For this part of the workshop, he gets the groups to come up with a single energy management intervention that would help the team.

One of the groups decides to institute a 10-minute break every 90 minutes. They have fun coming up with reenergizing activities they could do during those 10-minute breaks, such as taking short walks, listening to their favourite songs, doing some sudoku puzzles or even juggling.

The second group comes up with a plan for each individual to get a half-hour break sometime during the afternoon. "We call it the siesta plan," one of them says with an easy chuckle.

The third group—the group with Jillian in it—approaches KC for tips on how to bring energy levels down when things have gotten too frantic.

"One of the best exercises I know for that kind of situation is a breathing technique called centring. I use it with elite athletes before big competitions, such as the Olympics. It has amazing results."

The rest of the morning passes quickly and productively. By the end of the workshop, KC is satisfied with how things have gone.

"I think it's really helping," Dominic says to him as they gather up the markers and flip charts.

"It's helping everyone but Henri, it seems," Karen says. "Maybe the three of us could meet up to discuss how to deal with him."

Dominic nods energetically at this proposition, excited at the prospect of making some progress—any kind of progress—with Henri. "That'd be great. Just great. We need to do something about him."

"We'll sort it out," Karen says.

"But you know, I can see that this is really benefiting the group as a whole. I'd love to schedule another session, KC—the sooner, the better."

The optimist in KC wants to agree to another session right away.

It's a good group of people, and he'd love to keep up the momentum they've created today. But then he takes a minute to think about his schedule and realizes that the earliest time he's available isn't for another 10 days. The day after tomorrow, he's flying out west to Edmonton for a one-week training camp with the national women's basketball team. They're gearing up for the world championships in Istanbul in a few months, and it's his job to make sure they're mentally prepared to win.

He explains the situation to Dominic and Karen and suggests they schedule another session for when he gets back from Edmonton.

"Sure, sure, sounds great," says Karen.

"We'll be waiting," says Dominic.

CHAPTER 5

TRAINING CAMP

In this chapter, KC meets with the basketball coaches, and they talk about introversion, skill transfer to game situations and the TAIS, the Attentional and Interpersonal Style Inventory. There is also beer involved. It is a coaches' meeting.

Sitting in a window seat on the plane to Edmonton, KC feels excited about his trip. For the next week, he'll get to immerse himself in the world of sports. He likes the variety of his so-called job, but his work in sports has always lit a special fire in his soul. The pressure of competition, the thrill of a great performance, the rush of adrenaline—what a ride! But sports are also remarkably informative, one of the world's best learning grounds. In fact, he often thinks of sports as a laboratory for his work in the business world. Things are clear in sports. Things are easily measured. It's obvious when an intervention has worked and when it hasn't—the score will tell you. KC likes to say that a high jumper can tell you to an eighth of an inch how his day is going. That's a kind of clarity the rest of us don't always have.

He arrives at the airport and sees the smiling face of Donna, the team's national manager, waiting for him.

"Good flight?" she asks.

"No turbulence, no crash landings, no crying babies—can't really ask for more than that," he says.

"I don't know. I could always ask for a little more leg room," she replies with a smile as she leads him out to the car.

En route to the hotel, she gives him a quick rundown of how things are going with the team. It's familiar enough. Some players are playing well, and some are playing less well. A couple have specific issues they're hoping KC can help them sort out. All of them are adjusting to the new offensive and defensive schemes that the national team coaches have designed. With the world championships just a few months away, they're scheduled to play a couple of exhibition games versus Brazil at the end of the week in order to help them determine exactly where they are.

When Donna drops KC off at the hotel, he heads up to his room and quickly empties his suitcase. Tomorrow he has a session with the players. He's not yet sure what he wants to do with them or what they most need, but he's hoping he'll gain some clarity over dinner tonight. He's meeting up with the coaching staff—Wendy and Sean, the assistant coaches, and Linda, the new head coach of the team. He hasn't had the chance to meet Linda yet, but he's looking forward to remedying that this evening. After a quick 10-minute rest, he makes his way back downstairs to the hotel restaurant for dinner.

In the restaurant, he sees that Linda is the only one who's arrived. Although they haven't met face-to-face, he's followed her career and recognizes her straight away from dozens of pictures and videos he's seen.

"It's a pleasure to meet you," she says, rising to greet him. "I've never worked with a sports psychologist, but I'm sure looking forward to it. Everyone speaks so highly about you. Mike, especially, couldn't stop singing your praises."

Mike is the coach of the women's national hockey team. KC worked with the hockey players for years and helped them win back-to-back Olympic gold medals. In that time, he developed a great relationship with Mike, and the mention of this old friend brings a smile to KC's face.

"I've heard great things about you too," he says. "You've built up quite an impressive coaching history in a short time. As for Mike, you know how those hockey coaches like to exaggerate."

"Well, yeah. I was a bit skeptical when he suggested you walked on water," she says with a laugh. "But seriously, he's a great coach. And he can be a tough nut. So I figured if he likes the idea of sport psychology, there must really be something to it."

Linda's openness to the discipline is a welcome discovery. One of the big problems KC encountered earlier in his career was wasting too much time and energy helping players deal with a negative coach who resisted the whole process of sport psychology. It's hard for athletes to move to high-performance levels when they're forced to spend much of their energy just dealing with their coach. It is good to know that won't be the case with Linda and her staff.

He's just about to express this sentiment, when he looks up to see Sean and Wendy arriving at the table. Greetings float around as the latecomers take their seats, and within a few minutes, the waiter arrives to take their drink and dinner orders. After that, it's not long before the conversation turns to what it always turns to with a bunch of coaches: the game.

In terms of energy management, basketball is an interesting game; it's fast paced and involves starts and stops and constant movement up and down the court. But there's also precision involved, acute control of movement and energy. Good defence requires constant pressure on the ball and continuous communication between all five players. The only time one gets a break is when the ball is well away from the player he or she is guarding. But even then, a small lapse in energy and focus, even just a split second's lapse, can create a gap that someone slides through to—*swish*—score a basket.

On the offensive side of things, one needs huge bursts of energy to make a drive to the basket and power up for a shot. But the act of shooting calls for a softer touch and some finesse. KC remembers a famous coach's description of the difference between professional and college-level players: "The younger players jump as high as they can for every rebound, whereas the pros only jump as high as the ball."

This ability to quickly adjust energy levels for the desired occasion is key. Golfer Jack Nicklaus once wrote an article on how he managed his energy on each hole he played. He brought his energy level way up for his tee shot, but then he intentionally took it down as he walked to his ball. For the next shot, he brought it back up, and then he let it come down again. His energy level went up and down as required by the hole. KC often has his athletes assign a number from 1 to 10 to the ideal energy level for whatever they're doing. In the golfing example, Nicklaus might be at an eight or nine for his initial drive but at a five or six for his approach shot. His energy level might be even lower, maybe a three or a four, for his putt. For this energy-level control to be possible, players have to be able to monitor their arousal levels and adjust them.

Before KC and the other coaches get a chance to delve into how things are progressing with the basketball team, the waiter returns with the drinks—beers all around. Talk about adjusting energy levels!

"Cheers," says Linda, clinking her glass against the others'. "Good to have you with us, Kenneth."

"Should we toast something?" asks Sean.

"Of course we should! Let's toast the world-championship team," suggests Wendy.

"That'd be an idea," says Sean. "Except we haven't actually selected the team yet. We're still working that out."

"That's right," says Linda. "And it's causing the players a lot of stress. They're all competing for spots. Actually, Kenneth, this is just one of a handful of stressors we're battling at the moment."

"What are the others?"

"Well, let's see. The players also don't know each other well. They're playing with people they don't normally play with. Added to that, we don't have a lot of time together—there's a lot of pressure to make sure we use the time we have really well. And of course, we've got the world championships coming up. Our performance there will have a huge effect on whether or not we qualify for the Olympics."

As Linda runs through this list of concerns, KC notes that

the situation here is strikingly similar to the situation at Optimal IT. The players are all talented, high-level performers, not unlike the programmers at the tech company. Like the programmers, the players are trying to integrate new systems and ways of doing things into a team of people they have no history with. The programmers at Optimal IT don't have the pressure of Olympic qualifications, but their work is their livelihood. KC figures that maybe the psychological exercises and techniques that work best here with the team will work well with the programmers back at home. Once again, the world of sports can function as a little laboratory for KC's corporate work.

"Let's toast to a productive week then," Sean says.

They all raise their glasses in good cheer and enjoy the first few sips of beer.

"On that note," says Wendy, a former national team player herself, "in the spirit of a productive week, let me mention an issue we're having with the team. The players execute drills perfectly in practice. They're just great. But the minute we start a scrimmage, it's like the drills never happened. They don't execute the same way in games. What's that about? How do we fix that?"

It's a question KC has been asked a hundred times in a hundred different ways over the years: Why can't athletes perform at the same level in a game situation as they do in practice? On the one hand, it seems like a question with a simple answer: it's a psychological issue. If players are able to execute a manoeuvre in the morning but not in the evening, the problem isn't physical. The question is also about the transferability of a skill from one situation to an entirely different one—from practice to competition.

Often, coaches operate on the belief that if individuals work on a part of something judiciously and in isolation, that part will miraculously transfer into high-performance situations during game-day play. But there's a difference between *part* and *whole* learning. Figuring out how to perform a small part of the whole—out of context—doesn't necessarily mean that skill will transfer when everything is eventually pieced together into a complete game situation. In reality, the smaller the piece, the less the likelihood of transfer.

Years ago, swim coaches used to have their athletes perform drills on the deck of the pool. However, when these athletes got into the water and tried to execute the same patterns, they discovered the drills were virtually useless. The drills discounted the variables actually involved in swimming—like the water.

Of course, coaches have gotten better at drilling with bigger parts of the whole. The pick-and-roll basketball drill, in which players practice game-like shooting, is a big-enough piece of the game to allow for transferability. In such cases, where you can expect transferability, there's another problem at work—a familiar problem.

"Really, what we're talking about here is an energy management issue," KC says. "The players see the drill as a low-energy-level situation, a learning situation. But in a scrimmage, there's an expectation of performance, so they're working with different energy levels."

One of KC's favourite books on this subject is Dr. Sian Beilock's *Choke*. In it, Beilock discusses how pressure causes athletes to worry, which, in turn, causes them to try to control their performances. Unfortunately, this control and attention to performance can have a negative effect on their execution. In pressure-filled situations, athletes often try to think their way through things the way they did when they were in the learning stages of the sport.

KC summarizes her point for the coaches: "Under pressure, players often revert to what I call 'beginner's brain.'"

"I'm not sure what that means exactly," Wendy says.

"Let me put it this way: if you've ever played golf, you know what happens when you start to think through the parts of your swing instead of letting it be automatic. The learning part—the thinking part—should happen on the driving range, not while you're playing your round of golf."

"Right. Okay."

"I'm not suggesting we shouldn't put players under the mild pressure of scrimmage. Heck, research shows that's the only way for them to get better at handling pressure. But we also need to help them come up with strategies that keep them in the backs of their brains when it's game day. When I work with golfers, I sometimes have them hum a little song to themselves while they're setting up to hit a ball."

"Hum therapy," jokes Sean.

Wendy cracks a smile, but Linda ignores this little joke—KC's example seems to have set off a light in her head, and she's eager to add to the discussion. "Boy, that's something that might work for free-throw shooting. I remember reading that the coach Phil Jackson had his players chew gum during free-throw shots so that they'd stay relaxed."

"Gum therapy," Sean says, chiming in again.

This time, Linda succumbs to a light chuckle.

KC also indulges in a quick laugh before he carries on. "Yeah, exactly. That's the sort of thing I'm talking about. But we've got to remember that each player will have her own way of lowering her arousal level. What works for one person won't necessarily work for another. We need to work with them individually to help them find their flow in game situations."

As they sip their way through their beers, Sean considers what KC has said. His forehead crinkles with concentration. He's puzzled about something. "Kenneth, you said this was an energy management problem. What makes you sure of that?"

"To be completely accurate, it's an attentional issue," KC says. "And it's caused by increased arousal level, which is what makes it an energy management problem. When people's arousal levels are too high, their attentional focuses start to narrow, and they aren't able to take in critical information they need to perform well."

This explanation doesn't clear things up to Sean's satisfaction. His brow retrains its strange contortion for the moment.

To help him understand, KC comes at the issue from a slightly different direction. "One of the ways you'll know it's an energy management issue is if you correct one part of the action—let's say the angle at which you want them to drive off the screen. So they do that part correctly, but then they make a new mistake with something else—something they'd been doing just fine earlier. You start to feel like you're always in correction mode, like it's all falling apart."

"Like that never happens!" says Linda with a laugh of recognition. "Sometimes I get one thing working, but then the minute I try to add something to the working piece, something else goes wrong. It's like playing a game of Whac-a-Mole."

"It really is," affirms Wendy.

"And, Kenneth, you're saying this can all be traced back to a shortage of humming?" says Linda with a sly smile. "We aren't doing enough to promote the hum?"

"Or the gum!" adds Sean.

Linda laughs and touches KC warmly on the elbow, letting him know this is just a bit of leg pulling. Her laughter trails off as the waiter returns, this time carrying plates of delicious-looking pasta that smells as if it came straight out of an Italian mother's kitchen. The conversation breaks up for a few minutes while they make dents in their food, but KC's mind is still turning over the issue at hand.

"I know what you mean about a game of Whac-a-Mole, Linda," he says. "I think the problem here is that the players aren't taking the time to integrate what you're teaching them into the whole. They're overemphasizing the part that you're correcting. Here's a metaphor: it's like they're playing music out of tempo. You say the drums are too loud, so they control that. But then the string section goes wonky. It's simply a matter of taking a minute to rehearse the execution of the whole orchestra in their minds. I tell athletes to replay the correction the coach has just made and then replay it as just one part of the entire thing they're trying to execute. In that way, they stand a better chance of not overemphasizing the correction. Too often, we, as coaches, don't give them the time to step back and mentally do something before they have to physically do it."

"Is this what you're going to talk to the players about tomorrow?" asks Sean, digging into a big plate of spaghetti.

"Sure. At least in part. But I haven't entirely decided what I'm going to talk about yet. Might be good to hear some of your other concerns. What else is going on?"

"Well, there is something I think you need to address," Linda says. "Last night, the national volleyball team, the men's team, was playing here in town. It's a series of exhibition matches, and our team went over to watch. Well, most of our team did, which brings me to the issue: Farah didn't go. She's always the one who takes a pass on voluntary team activities. She plays a pivotal leadership role on the floor, so I don't think not participating in these activities is the best example to set."

KC scours his memory, trying to place Farah. "I think I remember her from junior camp. About five foot seven, long black hair, very quick? A point guard with a ton of potential?"

"That's Farah all right," says Wendy.

"Tell me about her. What's she like on a daily basis? Is she hard to get along with?"

"Oh no," all three coaches say in chorus.

"No, no, not at all," Linda says.

"She's about as nice a player as I've ever coached," says Wendy, and the others nod in agreement.

KC considers the situation for a moment and reaches a conclusion: "Then she must be introverted."

"Probably true," says Linda. "Getting her to communicate in a team meeting or even on the floor is like pulling teeth. But how did you know that?"

"If she's not a grumpy, moody sort of person, there has to be another reason for her not wanting to participate in social activities. Introverts find socializing exhausting. They need time alone to rest and recover. Now, I know that's hard for a bunch of extroverted coaches to imagine. Highly extroverted people constantly misread introverts as moody or distant, when really, all they're looking for is a little time alone to recharge their batteries. Those batteries get drained by social engagements. In Farah's case, the drain is probably pretty intense."

The pull and twist of concentration returns to Sean's brow. He's a man whose thoughts are clearly visibly on his face. When he's thinking something through, it's apparent. "Hmm. If we're misreading her, then chances are, so are the other women on the team. That's maybe something we should address. Could be the source of some tensions."

KC couldn't agree more. The importance of players understanding each other's needs is critical for the gelling of the team as a whole. "One of the things we'll do in the lead-up to the world championships, once you've selected the final team, is have everybody complete the TAIS inventory."

"TAIS? What's that stand for?" asks Sean.

"The Attentional and Interpersonal Style inventory. It's a psychological assessment I use with all the teams I work with. I'll meet with each of the players individually to go over their profiles so they understand themselves, how they pay attention and their attentional strengths and weaknesses. But we'll also do a team session to help the players understand each other. Here, each player will stand up and, in her own way, summarize her profile for the rest of the team."

"Don't you think they'll be reluctant to do that?" asks Linda.

"Some of them might be, sure," says KC. "But it's really no big deal. Like I said, I've done it with every team I've ever worked with. Players really need to understand the needs of their teammates, especially their pre-game needs. Some players need to sit in a corner with a towel over their heads. And those who don't need that often misread what's going on. This kind of misreading can really influence the whole team's energy level."

"Makes sense," says Linda. "But it's going to take courage to get some of these girls to stand up and speak in front of their teammates."

"That's true—so true. Courage is a big part of helping to lead a team. In presenting their profiles, some of these women will already be demonstrating tremendous courage. But we won't stop there. After each player presents her profile, the other players will give her feedback on what she's put forward. I'll speak to them before we start to the exercise and tell them a bit about how to give effective feedback. One of the rewards of presenting your profile is to get the feedback from your teammates. It creates incredibly strong bonds between the players."

"I can totally see that," says Wendy. "I'd have loved doing something like that back when I played. Would have helped so much. So what are we waiting for? Shouldn't we get this going right away?"

"I think it's probably best to do this after the world-championship team has been selected. That's the team that needs bonding. I mean, my understanding is that there are a few players who might be part of the final team who aren't even here at the moment, because they're playing with their professional teams in Europe. Isn't that the case?"

"Yeah, that's right," says Linda. "It's hard to get everyone together."

"So the exercise might be a bit premature at the moment."

"Right, right," says Wendy.

As the conversation tips toward a lull, KC finally gets a chance to look down at his plate of spaghetti. He's barely touched it—not because it's not delicious but because he's been too busy talking, lost in conversation. This is typical. It's easy for KC to get so wrapped up in interesting discussions that he forgets to eat. Or drink. Or call his wife.

He refocuses on his dinner, as everyone does. Once they're all working their way through their last bites of spaghetti and last sips of beer, KC feels his energy start to dip. The effects of the flight, the time change and the big pasta dinner become harder and harder to fight off. As if on cue, Linda raises one final issue the team's been facing: fatigue.

"There's no shortage of fatigue during the training-camp week," she says. "The players are constantly complaining of it. And yet when they're given a day off, they don't use it to rest and recover. Instead, they do all the fun social things they've been missing out on because of the intense schedule."

KC is not surprised. Most people don't understand how much rest time they need, and they don't understand what real rest is. The old expression "A change is as good as the rest" might work with people who are bored and need to be energized, but it doesn't work with those who are fatigued. Some benefits can only by reaped by sleeping and getting some solid rest. In fact, his own need for a good stretch of sleep is rapidly taking hold of him.

"You've got Chris working with the players in camp, right?" he asks.

"We do."

"Is he doing any urine samples or blood tests? If he is, he can easily identify the players' levels of fatigue. I worked with the world junior championships in hockey a few years back, and one of our coaches used to let the athletes know every two days how they were doing in terms of their energy recovery systems—from a purely physiological perspective. That's something we might want to speak to Chris about. The guy who worked with us on the women's hockey team had an interesting system involving electrodes. Either of those systems might help us here."

"Measuring with electrodes has been pretty successful, hasn't it? I mean, I've heard a lot of winning teams have used that system," says Wendy.

"It's complicated in its workings but easy to use."

KC goes on to explain that the system analyzes different parameters of the body to determine a person's readiness for activity. The athlete wears a special heart-rate monitor that includes an ECG (electrocardiogram) and two electrodes on the thumb and forehead. She lies down for five minutes and relaxes while the system reads the physiological readiness of the central nervous system, cardiovascular system and energy-supply system. Using its algorithm, the program then classifies the player as red (meaning she should stop because she needs recovery), yellow (meaning she can proceed but should modify her behaviour) or green (meaning she's good to go). The main measure is the balance or imbalance of the parasympathetic and sympathetic nervous systems. Different protocols can then be used to help the athletes maintain a better balance—either more recovery-based work, if their systems are taxed and more sympathetic dominant, or more intervals to kickstart their parasympathetic systems.

"Wow, that sounds pretty space-agey," says Wendy.

"It does seem like a weird sci-fi experiment," says Sean.

"But if it helps, I'm on board," says Linda. "How exactly do coaches use the information?"

"If there's a team-wide energy issue—for example, if the team's been on the road for a while and players haven't been getting adequate rest—this system will let you know. Then we can modify practice and work in short bursts. That's how we did it with the women's hockey team. When I worked with them at the Sochi Olympics, we had five veteran players, and sometimes they just needed a day off, because they didn't recover as quickly as the younger players."

"Were the players all right with that? With taking a day off?"

"They're all very competitive—that's for sure. So initially, there were some objections from the veterans. They didn't want to take days off. But they soon saw the wisdom in it. And after taking those days off, their bodies validated the decision. They performed at a way higher level. In the end, they embraced it," says KC, breaking into a yawn on the last few words.

Linda takes a look at her watch and says, "It's getting late. We'd better not violate the very principles we're talking about. Let's all get to bed and pick back up tomorrow. Fresh eyes, fresh minds, fresh bodies."

"As an old veteran, I really appreciate that intervention," says KC with a tired smile. "This elder needs some shut-eye."

CHAPTER 6

SESSION WITH THE PLAYERS

In this chapter, KC introduces the players to some key concepts in energy management: active awareness, choking, ABC energy management, centring, and acting as if you have time.

The following morning, fresh after a good night's rest, KC heads over to the gymnasium complex, where he'll meet with the players in a small conference room near the basketball courts. The players are used to these sessions, and they look forward to them because these meetings give them a chance to talk about their experiences and what they're going through and to vent about the coaches who seem difficult and demanding. KC often sees himself as a neutral corner to which the players or coaches can go to get things off of their chests. Everyone knows that what he or she says to KC goes no further than him.

KC gets to the conference room with about 15 minutes to spare. However, he's not the first to arrive. He's delighted to see Monique, one of the veteran players, already floating around. One of the first things KC learned about Monique is that she's a world-champion hugger. As soon as she spots him entering the room, she says, "I need my morning hug."

KC laughs and obliges her with a hug. He's always liked Monique. They've had some great conversations over the years about fitness and running. Running is a shared hobby of theirs, and Monique is an exceptional runner. She still runs road races in the off-season. The activity keeps her in terrific shape, but sometimes it also means she overtrains. Overtraining is a tendency of hers. She's one of the hardest workers on the team, always spending time in the weight room, attending yoga classes or firing through her training sessions with Chris.

Her work ethic is admirable, but when she gets injured, the injury is almost always a result of overuse. If Chris suggests, for example, that 15 pull-ups are great for a basketball player's upper-body strength, Monique is likely to do 25 or 30.

"There's no question that exercise is a healthy prescription," KC has told her in the past. "But if I tell you to take one aspirin, that doesn't mean taking the whole bottle is better."

Monique's greatest strengths—her drive, determination and ability to push herself—easily become weaknesses, because she takes everything to the extreme. She knows this, but she gets caught up in the training sessions anyway.

"How are you doing today, Monique?" KC asks.

"Not bad. My hip's a bit sore—evidence of that brutal squat session Chris had us do the other day."

"Were you overdoing it again?"

"I really tried not to! As soon as I noticed the discomfort in my hip, I stopped right away. I can't afford an injury."

"I'm so glad to hear that, Monique. You know, I read an article the other day that might interest the runner in you."

"Oh yeah? I'm all ears."

"The author points out that most people who run do it because they love it. So taking time off isn't usually high on their list of priorities. However, he goes on to point out that taking a few days off not only can help your performance but also won't decrease your fitness level. Turns out that a break from running—a break of less than two weeks—isn't likely to affect your fitness level in any dramatic way. But not taking rest days will certainly affect your performance. You always want to make sure you recover more than you actually think you need to."

"This is something I've been realizing," says Monique. "I'm not getting any younger. It's always taking me longer to recover from injuries."

"The thing that really hit me in this article is that your body doesn't get stronger and faster during runs. The improvements to fitness come during the recovery stage, when your body goes to work repairing the damage done during the workout."

Monique is quiet for a moment while she reflects on this concept. Then she says, "Huh. That's a neat way to think about it. The only way to get fit is to allow full recoveries. Thanks, KC. That's a helpful perspective."

"I thought you might like that. And while we're on the subject, I read another great article on the joys of running, and it was—"

There's no telling how long this conversation could spiral on, but just then, Sharon enters the room and, with a smile, says, "What conspiracies are you two coming up with?"

"Something much bigger than world domination," quips Monique. "We're trying to figure out how to make you a usable power forward, and quite frankly, we're stumped."

Sharon is saved from having to make a witty retort by the arrival of the other players, who now quickly fill out the room. It's time for the session to begin.

"Last time I was here, we did some great work on awareness," KC says to the team.

Awareness is the foundation of good energy management. Without an awareness of what's going on with your energy levels, there's no hope of controlling them. Given its importance, KC decides to begin the session with a quick review of this foundational aspect.

In discussions of awareness, KC always points out the three different parts of ourselves that require our awareness. These parts all have something in common: they can be observed by the self. At the top of a piece of chart paper, KC writes *SELF* in big block letters.

"You'll remember from our last session that we talked a bit about the self. It's the self that notices things."

"The self is the observer," says Jessica. "I remember you saying that last time."

"Right. The self is the observer," he echoes. "I'm glad to see someone was paying attention last time, Jessica."

"Do I get a gold star or something?" she jokes.

"I'm fresh out of stickers. But you do get a leg up on mental fitness."

"I'll take it!"

With a quick smile, KC turns his attention back to the chart paper. Farther down the page, he draws three ovals on a level. In the first, he writes the word *Body*; in the second, he writes *Feelings*; and in the last, he writes *Mind*. The self can notice and observe all three of these elements.

Pointing to the first of these ovals, KC says, "We all know that the self can become aware of what's going on at the body level. What are some examples of that?"

"An increase in heart rate?" says Keisha, one of the new players.

"Sure, exactly," says KC.

"Or like, sweaty palms?" volunteers Lynn, a sweet but nervous young woman. Sweaty palms are something she's familiar with.

"Right. Both great examples of things we notice at the body level. Now, how about feelings?" he asks, pointing to the middle oval on the chart paper. "What can the self notice on a feelings level, an emotional level?"

"Frustration," says one voice.

"Anger," says another.

"Disappointment."

"Regret."

"Bitterness."

"Fear."

"Okay, okay, what a happy bunch you all are today!" KC says.

Some of the girls laugh, realizing the list they've spontaneously generated skews a little negative.

"But I think everyone gets the idea," says KC. He gestures to the last oval. "So what about this last one, the mind? How does the self observe the mind?"

This one is a little tougher—KC knows this. People often think of the mind itself as being the observer. But the mind—and the thoughts that enter it—can be observed, just as the body and the feelings can be observed. This is a fact that KC is reminded of every time he meditates.

This concept of the mind as distinct from the self puzzles another of the new players, Sarah. "Are you saying that I'm not my mind? That it isn't my mind that observes what's going on?"

"Let me ask you this, Sarah," KC says. "Have you ever been trying to fall asleep, but you can't quite get your mind to stop racing? You're telling your mind to shut up. But it just won't?"

"Yes, I guess so," she stammers, red-faced, looking around the room nervously, uncomfortable to be put on the spot.

But there's no need for discomfort. Almost all of the other players are nodding, and some are even chuckling to themselves at the familiarity of this scenario.

KC says, "Well, you're not alone. Take a look at the body language in the room right now. It seems like everyone recognizes this particular experience. The question you've got to ask is this: *Who* is telling the mind to shut up?"

"The self?"

"Right. Your self. Being aware of what's going on at the body, feelings and mind levels is really going to help you manage your energy. Which brings us right to the heart of what I want to talk about today: energy management."

The players sit up a little taller, the way they always do when new concepts are about to be introduced to them.

"We're going to start by talking about what happens in situations when your energy level is too high, when your arousal level is overly elevated and when you don't perform as well as you'd like."

"You mean we're going to talk about choking. But you don't want to call it that," says Sharon, one of the veterans. Sharon's a strong athlete with a fiery personality. She likes to call things as they are. It's a quality the other players usually appreciate, and today is no exception. They laugh at her quick unveiling of KC's attempted euphemism.

"Okay, you got me," says KC. "That's exactly what we're going to talk about—choking."

"Awesome. Choking is a problem I could really do without," Sharon says.

One of the things KC loves about working with athletes is their directness and honesty. They face right up to things. It's how they've gotten to be where they are—on a national team.

"Let's do a bit of an exercise to start. I want you to come up with a list of things that happen at the body, feelings and mind levels when your hot buttons are pushed. Basically, what are the clearest signals you're aware of that let you know your energy is getting too high?"

Keisha is again eager to offer a response. "I always raise my shoulders when I'm overenergized. They get all tight," she says.

"Good. What else?"

"When I'm upset, my breathing gets pretty shallow," says Raquel.

"I get a sort of panicky feeling sometimes. Almost like dread," someone else says.

"I know I'm getting worked up when I start yelling at myself in my head," another voice adds.

"Oh yeah, me too," says Sarah. "I do that all the time—yell at myself."

The women continue this exploration of their triggers for several minutes, and when their brainstorming begins to taper out, KC explains how important it is to be able to identify these signals when they arise. It's a critical component of what he calls the Early Warning System.

"Noticing, for example, at the body level that your shoulders are high—as you mentioned, Keisha—is like an oil light coming on in your car. It tells you something is wrong, and you should take action. But remember—the warnings aren't always physical. Sometimes you may notice a strong feeling of uncertainty, fear or dread—someone mentioned dread. This is information that tells you you're not in your ideal performance state. You need to adjust something."

"Okay, but so how exactly do we adjust things?" asks Monique. "I can usually tell I'm getting upset. But I don't know how to fix it. That's my problem."

KC's favourite example of a good energy management procedure is how paramedics are able to handle high-intensity situations. Paramedics operate with a two-step procedure: (1) check for hazards (e.g., fire, wire, glass, gas) and (2) check ABC (i.e., airway, breathing and circulation). With a simple, quick and automatic procedure, it's easier to ensure that the medics do the right things in the heat of a stressful situation.

"Like the paramedics, you want to establish a simple, repeatable two- or three-step process that you can deploy—a process that will help you regain your calm and return you to an ideal performance state."

"Okay. That sounds good. But what exactly is this process? What are the steps?" says Monique.

Typical Monique, thinks KC. Monique is a problem solver, a workhorse. She likes to get down to the bottom of things, identify the trouble and find ways to fix it. This attitude can make her a great force on the team, but it also means she gets frustrated easily when solutions aren't clear to her.

KC says, "We'll take some time later to come up with a personalized process for each of you. Everyone is different, and everyone can draw on the techniques that work best for her. But right now, I'm going to go over two general skills that will help you bring your energy down. The first is centring. The second is acting as if you have time."

"I think I've heard about centring. It's a relaxation technique, right?" says Jessica.

"Right. It's a way of triggering what's called your relaxation response."

As KC explains to the team, a Harvard doctor, cardiologist Herbert Benson, discovered the relaxation response in 1974. Benson conducted studies on people who were excellent at relaxing themselves. These were people who practiced meditation or used what we've now come to call autogenic training or other physical relaxation methods. These individuals were capable of getting into deep, trancelike states—world-champion relaxers. Benson hooked them all up to biofeedback equipment and made some interesting discoveries.

"What Benson found was that no matter what method these people were using to relax, they all went to the same place," KC says.

"Wow," says Samantha with exaggerated awe. "Like teleportation? Where did they all go?"

KC has always encouraged humour in his sessions. He claims he's learned more in a pub than he's ever learned in a classroom, and he credits that learning to the spirit of fun that exists around a pub table. But right now, he's not sure if Samantha is joking around or if she's asking a serious, honest-to-goodness question about teleportation. He pauses, a bit uncertain how to respond, but then he catches a mischievous glint in her eye.

"Okay, Sam, I'll admit you had me for a second there. I was beginning to think that the concussion you had last year had a deeper impact than we realized," he says.

Samantha playfully taps her head and says, "All good here. At least I think so."

"Good. Then let me get back on track. The place I'm referring to—the place all these champion relaxers went to—is only physical in the sense that it's located in the primitive part of the brain. Very close to the flight-or-fight response, actually. Now, I'm sure you're all familiar with the flight-or-fight response. It gets engaged when we're being reactive, when we're heading into that choker's profile. We're very good at firing up this response. But there's also a relaxation response in the brain. And when we trigger this, our respiration falls dramatically, our heart rate goes down—"

"Sounds a lot like sleep," interrupts Samantha.

"Yes. But it's much deeper than sleep. Learning how to trigger this relaxation response will allow you not only to lower your energy when it's too high but also to regain energy. It refuels you."

"Wait, wait, wait. Let me make sure I'm getting this," says Samantha. "You're telling us that inside our brains, there's an area we can trigger that's basically prewired to respond to that trigger by deeply relaxing us? Is that true? Can that be true? I feel like if I had this response, I'd be way more relaxed way more often."

"You absolutely would be—if you knew how to trigger it."

"Hm."

Samantha looks puzzled, even skeptical. To help persuade her, KC offers a tidy analogy: "Think about it this way. You might have a computer that has a ton of functions, but if you don't know what buttons to push to engage those functions, having them is pretty much pointless."

"So how do we trigger it?" asks Monique, still single-mindedly focused on the specifics, on the solution. "With this centring stuff? What is it exactly?"

Before KC details the centring relaxation technique, he has a question for the players. He wants to gauge their previous experience with relaxation exercises. "How many of you went through some type of a relaxation class with your team sports psychologist when you were in university?" he asks.

Most of the players raise their hands or nod. KC expected as much. Relaxation exercises are common in high-level university sports.

"Looks like most of you," he says. "That's great. What was the experience like?"

Keisha shoots up a hand and says, "Normal. But also weird."

"What do you mean? What was normal? What was weird?" he asks.

"Well, hmm, the normal part was how simple it was. We all lay down in the room, and Susan, our sports psychologist, had us focus on different parts of our body. We started with our toes and moved all the way up to our faces. She'd say things like 'Your legs are getting heavy,' or 'Feel the tension in your shoulders release.' Things like that. That was all pretty normal. But in a few minutes, my whole body was so relaxed I wasn't sure I could even move it. That was the weird part."

At this point, Sharon jumps in. "Yeah, I've done that too. It was cool and everything. But I can't see how we're going to use that in the middle of a game. What do we do—call a timeout and have everybody lie on the floor?"

"No, that might not be the best idea," KC agrees. "But the centring technique is a terrific miniprocedure you can use before and even during big games."

KC has long been convinced of the merits of the centring technique, which was developed in the martial art aikido. He's seen elite athletes across a spread of sports use this technique to lower their resting heart rates by more than 50 beats in just a few breaths. It's a simple procedure with a three-step progression. Its simplicity is part of what he likes about it.

"The first step of centring is to focus on the diaphragm—the muscle below the rib cage—as you breathe in. So let's all try this together. Let's stand up."

The players jump up to their feet, keen to be doing something more active than sitting at tables.

"Okay. Now breathe in, focusing one hundred percent on your diaphragm." KC pauses while the women take deep breaths. "Good. Now hold the air for a second, and then let it go. *Let* is the key word here. Just release the air. There's no pushing, just allowing."

KC waits for the players to slowly exhale. When they've done this, they look at him expectantly.

"Okay. The second step is a progression of the first. Again, I want you to breathe in and focus on the diaphragm. But this time, as you exhale, shift your attention to your shoulders, and let them relax. Then bring your attention to your knees. Let them bend slightly."

KC watches the wave of focused inhalations pass through the team. He sees shoulders drop perceptibly and knees adopt a slight bend. He sees relaxation.

"Now grab a partner," he says. "We're going to practice this in pairs. But first, Samantha, would you mind coming up here to help me demonstrate?"

Samantha springs to the front of the room with a mock bow

at the group. KC has her stand sideways so that the rest of the players have a profile view of her. Then he places his left hand on her shoulder and his right hand on her diaphragm. "You'll start by doing the first two steps, just as we talked about. So, Sam, focus on your diaphragm; focus on making my right hand extend outward on your inhalation. And then focus on your shoulders falling—my hand falling—when you exhale."

KC has found that because athletes are so physical, giving them something physical to focus on, such as a hand on the shoulder, is helpful in accelerating the learning process.

"Now, the third step, the last step, is to make sure that your exhalation is longer than your inhalation. Anytime you exhale for longer than you inhale, your body begins to relax. This time, Sam, count out your inhalation, and see if you can make your exhalation twice as long."

Samantha inhales deeply, moving KC's right hand outward. When she exhales, she slows things down, allowing this part of her breath to lengthen. After two cycles of this, she looks at KC, beaming. "Oh, wow! That really makes a huge difference. And it's something I could do quietly before I shoot a free throw."

"That's the idea. But you've got to be able to do this when you're already a little worked up. So let's practice it in a higher-energy situation. Everyone clap your hands seven times—as fast as possible," KC instructs.

The players break into what sounds like a round of forced applause, and the minute they finish, KC calls out, "Good. Now clap five times. Fast as you can!"

When they've completed this round, he adds, "Now three times. Fast, fast, fast!"

All of the movement and clatter has the expected effect on the players—the energy in the room has gone way up.

"Now become aware of your current energy level," KC says. "We've obviously brought it up quite a bit. I want you to practice the three-step centring technique to bring your arousal level back down."

KC watches the players work in pairs, one person focusing first on the inhalation and then on lengthening the exhalation while the other rests a hand on her partner's shoulder and diaphragm, as KC did with Samantha.

"It really works!" says Raquel with wide-eyed surprise after a few breaths.

KC smiles. He's always slightly amused at this kind of surprise and the skepticism it implies. "Glad to hear it, Raquel. But remember—this is a skill. And you need to treat it like any other skill. You need to practice it and get better at it."

"But we should be practicing it in high-arousal situations, right?" she asks.

"Great thinking. Absolutely. And you also want to try to incorporate it into your daily life. So think about your day yesterday. Were there places where you could have practiced this technique? Times when you would have liked to lower your arousal level?"

While Raquel thinks over his questions, Monique jumps in with an example of her own: "How about in the car? For the three of us who had to drive with Jessica? We had several near-death experiences. We could have practiced this technique then."

"Oh, come on. It wasn't that bad," says Jessica in her own defence. "There are a lot of bad drivers out there, especially the slow ones. I just had to get around them."

The players all laugh. Jessica's driving skills—or lack thereof—are legendary on the team. They've even started drawing straws to decide who gets stuck as a passenger in Jessica's car.

Sharon is quick to second Monique's suggestion. "As someone who was trapped in Jessica's death wagon yesterday, I can say I'd have loved to have brought my arousal level down. But you have to be standing up to do this centring stuff. It wouldn't be any good in a car."

"No, no," says KC quickly. "We've practiced it standing up. But it works just as well if you're sitting. When you're in a seated situation, instead of focusing on your knees bending a little at the end of your exhalation, you'd focus on your buttocks sinking into the seat. Anytime you're sitting or standing, you can practice this. That's the great thing about this skill. It's totally unobtrusive. No one knows you're doing it."

"I guess they wouldn't," says Sarah. "People expect you to breathe, after all."

The players spend a few more minutes identifying other opportunities for them to practice this skill in daily life. It's surprisingly easy for them to come up with options. After all, they don't need any extra time to practice it, and there's never any shortage of high-arousal situations in ordinary city life.

After a quick glance at his watch, KC brings the brainstorming to an end. "Okay, we're running low on time, which is actually maybe the perfect point to introduce the second skill I want to teach you: acting as if you have time."

"I don't know if we have time for that," someone jokes. "We've got practice in a few minutes. And I need a bathroom break."

KC slows down his movements, adjusts his posture and generally adopts a more-languorous demeanour, as if he's a man with all the time in the world, not a man with about five minutes left in his session and a lot of material he still wants to talk about.

"Look, we all know the mind informs the body," he says. "But the body also informs the mind. It's important to communicate your desires to yourself with congruent messages from both the mind and the body."

"We're talking about body language?" Jessica asks.

"Yes. We are."

"Another gold star!" she says.

"You're really racking up those imaginary stars today, Jess," says Sharon.

"I know. Isn't it great? I stick them on my imaginary reward chart. It's right next to all my imaginary Olympic gold medals. I'm visualizing."

The women share a quick laugh before KC draws their attention back to the matter at hand.

"Body language," he says. "We were talking about body language. Most research in this area focuses on the impact of your body language on those around you. But there's some great research all about the messages your body language is sending to you."

KC is thinking of one of his favourite researchers in the field,

Amy Cuddy. He describes her research for the team, studies that have shown how powerful an effect your own body language can have on you. Sitting in a power pose, for example, in which you make yourself open and big, increases your testosterone level and lowers your cortisol level. In essence, you're becoming stronger and more relaxed—not a bad combination for an athlete—and that's just if you assume the pose for a couple of minutes.

"What this research tells us is that there are real consequences to choosing to act *as if* something were the case—as if you're a power player, as if you're strong and confident, as if you have a lot of time. When you act *as if* and when you adopt the corresponding body language, what happens is you actually start to become what it is you're acting like. It's funny, but when you act as if you have time, it's amazing how much time you get! And this is important, because in high-arousal settings, one of the main sources of pressure is the perception that you don't have enough time. That leads to rushing. Acting as if you have time is a way of sending reassuring messages to yourself through your body language."

"Fake time to make time," Sharon says.

"I like it," says Jessica.

"Good. Because I want you all to try it the next time you're feeling rushed. We'll talk about this again later to see how the technique worked for you."

With that, KC wraps up the session. It's time for the players to head over to the basketball courts and start their practice. There's a buzz of conversation among the players as they leave the small conference room. KC recognizes this chatter as a sign that his session has hit home. This feeling is confirmed when he arrives at the gym a few minutes later and finds them all joking around and working on their power poses.

As KC watches the team warm up and observes the high spirits and light laughter, his thoughts drift to Optimal IT. This is the kind of atmosphere he'd like to help create there: focused, determined and competent but also lighthearted and fun. If there's any group that needs to learn to act as if they have time, it's the programmers at the tech company. They're forever saying that they don't have time and wish deadlines would be pushed back. They spend enormous amounts of time complaining about how little time they have! The acting-as-if-you-have-time technique might be an excellent concept to introduce to that group. This brief visit with the world of sports has, as usual, provided KC with some great inspiration.

Standing on the sidelines of the court, KC reflects on attitudes toward time and on the strange nature of time, the relativity of time. Many years ago, in a workshop, a woman once remarked to him that the length of a minute depends on which side of the bathroom door you're standing on.

"How true," he says to himself.

CHAPTER 7

MEANWHILE, BACK AT OPTIMAL IT

In this chapter, the IT team identifies demands and distractions and creates a single-focus plan.

KC has barely finished unpacking from his basketball trip when his cellphone rings. It's Karen.

"Hey there, jet-setter. How was the training camp?" she asks.

"Oh, great—just great."

"I trust you've got them whipped into shape and ready to rock at the world championship next month?"

"We're getting there. And it's a great team, a strong team."

KC begins to give her a quick summary of how things went at camp. He's just about to get going on all of the parallels he noticed between the basketball team and the programmers at Optimal IT when she interrupts him.

"I really am interested in all that, Kenneth, but I just got a text from Douglas Adams, our CEO, so I've only got a minute. He wants to meet with you."

"I'd love to meet him too."

Karen seems to barely hear him. She carries on. "And tomorrow you and I will be meeting with Dominic and three of his team members."

"Oh. I knew you and I were meeting tomorrow, but what made you decide to include the others? I know you don't do anything without some underlying plan. So tell me. What are you scheming?" he teases.

"Scheming? What does that mean? I'm not scheming anything," she says in an odd tone, almost as though his choice of word has offended her.

"Oh, I didn't mean to insult you. I was just trying to be funny," he says quickly, trying to smooth any ruffled feathers.

Karen responds just as quickly. "No, no, I'm the one who should apologize. It's just—it's been busy here. I've already had a full day, and now Douglas drops a bunch of new stuff on me out of the blue and expects me to put everything else aside. Often—actually, very often—by the time I present him with whatever it is he demanded I get done, he's already moved on to something else. It's like the thing that was so urgent yesterday hardly matters anymore today. Only I've been here stressing and straining about it."

"I'll be sure to raise this point with him when I meet him. It'll be the first thing I say to him," KC jokes, hoping to see her sense of humour return.

Her tone does lighten. "I can see why you work in psychology, Kenneth. That kind of confrontation would be the perfect way to kick off a relationship with him. You know, I rarely think of starting a relationship by detailing all the things the other person is doing wrong. Can hardly wait to see how it works out for you!"

KC laughs, glad to see that Karen's humour is still intact. "It'll be a surefire success."

"Well, you'll get your chance to test that tomorrow, because we're meeting with him fifteen minutes before our meeting with Dominic and the others."

KC would like to pepper her with questions about Douglas, but knowing she's pressed for time, he directs the conversation to his more-pressing concerns. "What do you want to get out of this meeting with Dominic? What are your goals here?"

"I thought we should do a bit of a needs assessment of the group. I'd like us to figure out their biggest issues so that our sessions can provide maximum value. I want to hit the nail squarely on the head."

"Totally agree. After all, our purpose here is to meet their needs. It's not to just provide them with material we think they ought to know. And based on what you've just told me about Douglas, I suspect they already get their fair share of extraneous exercises. It probably leads them to multitask—which, by the way, is a misnomer. It's a terrible thing."

"Hey, there's something else you could talk to Douglas about! Another great point of entry. Tell him how he's bringing the whole organization down."

"I can't imagine how that conversation could go wrong!"

"But you're absolutely right about him. The impact he has on the team is huge. When we were a smaller organization, he knew everybody, and he knew what everybody was doing. His interventions were always face-to-face, and they were typically very helpful. But with the expansion, that's just not how things are anymore."

"That's certainly something we can—"

"Hold that thought, Kenneth. I really do have to run right now. But I'll meet you at nine forty-five tomorrow morning. We'll meet in Douglas's office. It's on the first floor, just to the left of the main entrance. Flash the security badge I issued you last time you were here, and the front desk will let you right in. Now I really have to go."

Before he can say goodbye, Karen is off the line. He holds the disconnected phone in his hand and looks at it, thinking that the atmosphere over there must still be hectic. Nonetheless, he's looking forward to getting back into things at Optimal IT, and he's looking forward to meeting the man at the helm.

KC has been in his fair share of CEOs' offices, but he's never seen one like this. First and foremost, this one is remarkably unpretentious. It isn't guarded by legions of administrative staff. There's no outer office through which visitors must pass. Apart from the kindly receptionist at the front desk, to whom KC shows his security badge, there are no hurdles on his way to the CEO's office. There's just a door, partly ajar, with the name Douglas Adams stenciled on it in block letters. Heck, it's not even a fancy door; it's plain old wood.

Through the half-open door, KC hears Douglas talking on the phone. He waits until the call ends, and then he knocks on the door. *Tap-tap-tap.*

"Come in, Kenneth!" Douglas yells.

KC pushes the door wide open and steps inside. "How did you know it was me?" he asks.

Douglas motions to his office windows. "I see everyone who walks in the front door. I didn't recognize you, but I figured at this exact time, who else?" He strides across the room and extends his hand to KC. "Nice to meet you."

As KC shakes his hand, he thinks to himself that Douglas has what he refers to as a military handshake—firm, solid and businesslike, conveying a slight message of power and authority.

"That was Karen on the phone," Douglas says. "She's going to be ten minutes late—which is my fault, really, because I threw something at her last minute. But I'm happy to talk to you one on one anyway. Let me just find my notes."

Notes? thinks KC. *This man is prepared.* While Douglas rifles through some papers on his desk, KC looks around the office. A large golf trophy sits on one of the shelves. Other golf paraphernalia lies around it, and some of it looks autographed.

"You're a golfer, I see," KC says. "And from the looks of that trophy, a pretty successful one—there aren't many of those!"

Douglas spins around and follows KC's gaze to the trophy. His eyes crinkle happily, and the right corner of his mouth turns upward almost into a smile. "Well, I had a lucky few holes that day. If you golf at all, you know that repetition is the real challenge. Repeating a good shot and then a good hole and then a good round—well, that happens rarely. At least to me."

"I was always more of a tennis guy myself," says KC. "Or I was in my younger life. But in the last few years, I've taken up golf. So

I know just what you're talking about. I've almost never left the course feeling absolutely terrific about what I've done. The could-have-beens really get stuck in my head."

With this opening exchange, the two of them get swept up in a discussion of golf—golf courses, golfers and anything and everything related to that challenging and fascinating game. There's no telling how long the conversation might have pushed on if Karen hadn't at last walked through the door.

"I could hear you two all the way down the hall. I guess there's no end to how long two old duffers can talk golf," she teases.

"I object to your use of the word *old*. Kenneth and I are in our prime," Douglas says.

"That might be true of you, Douglas. But I'm afraid both *old* and *duffer* are pretty accurate descriptors of me."

"Well then, old duffer, take a seat."

The three of them sit down around a small table in a corner of Douglas's office. Douglas is commanding in his manner, completely assured. He's comfortable being in charge of things, and he guides the conversation as he likes.

"Let me start," he says. "I was going to say this before you got here, Karen, but we seem to have gotten a bit sidetracked by the little white ball. I'm going to be very honest with you both. When I first heard about your so-called energy management program, I was more than a little resistant to the idea. I was actually going to raise the issue with you, Karen, but I got caught up in other things, so that conversation kept getting delayed. And before I knew it, you'd already had your first session with Dominic's team.

"Now, I've known some of those guys for a long time, so I had a conversation with a few of them about the session. Initially, it made no sense to me at all to take time off to discuss this energy management stuff—not when time is so tight right now and they don't have any of it to waste. But I'll admit it—I got some really positive feedback. So I'm holding off my evaluation of the whole intervention until I see what it all yields. I understand you're meeting with some of Dominic's guys again this morning? What's that about?"

Douglas speaks quickly but clearly. As he directs this last question straight to Karen, his eyes are attentive, his eyebrows slightly raised.

"We want to make sure that we spend our time and resources as well as we can, so I thought it'd be a good idea to meet with some of the most-senior people. I want to do a bit of a needs assessment to understand what's what."

"I trust your instincts, Karen," says Douglas with a curt nod. "Even though I don't fully understand what you just said."

Karen starts to expand on the purpose of the meeting, trying to elucidate things for Douglas. However, he waves a hand at her, making it clear he doesn't want to hear any more.

"I don't need to know all the details just now. I've got another meeting." He rises from his chair and looks at his watch. "And I'm already seven minutes late. Just keep me posted. Kenneth, it was a pleasure. We'll have to schedule ourselves a golf game sometime."

Without waiting for a reply, Douglas breezes out of his office, leaving KC and Karen sitting inside.

For a moment, KC stares at the door through which Douglas passed, and then he looks at Karen with a shrug. "I'm not sure what just happened—or whether it's good news or bad news for our program."

She laughs and says, "It can only be good. Douglas is a very practical engineering type, so the fact that he's fine with us continuing is a good sign. And he obviously likes you. Good thing you opened the relationship by bonding over golf instead of your original plan to point out all the mistakes he was making in his management style," she teases.

"I reconsidered that plan. Found some flaws in it after all."

"Wise move," she says, and she rises and makes her way toward the office door. "Now we need to get going. We're going to be late."

She hurries on, hardly waiting for KC, who springs out of his chair and follows at her heels. Together they make their way to a conference room, where Dominic is already waiting, as are the three senior members of his team. KC recognizes them from his first session: Kate, Lucas and John.

"Sorry, sorry," Karen says, pulling out a seat at the table. "Douglas held us up a bit."

"Now, there's a shocking development. Our illustrious leader, Douglas, has thrown someone off their schedule!" says Kate.

It turns out Kate is one of the "guys" Douglas referred to. But it's clear from her tone and from the warmth with which they all joke about Douglas that they like the man. He must be doing some things right.

When they get into the business at hand, it's Dominic who opens up the conversation. "Things have been slightly better since our first session, Kenneth. I'm happy to report that. But the big question is this: How do we continue to make progress? Because we've still got a long way to go and a lot to do in the next few weeks."

Although he directs his question to KC, Karen undertakes an answer. "We're going to start with a needs assessment today to determine where you most need help and how we can be most effective."

As Karen gets her needs assessment underway, it becomes apparent that she's an incredibly gifted facilitator. KC isn't surprised by this. Everything he knows about her supports this discovery. She takes the group through a series of awareness exercises that help them—and KC—identify what the next steps ought to be. At one point, she puts the same question to each of them individually. She asks, "If you could do one thing differently—one thing that would make all the difference to your performance and work environment—what would it be?"

After a few minutes of reflection on this question, the team members toss around their thoughts and ideas. The responses seem to centre on the flood of distractors that keep them from delving into their work. Their problem is focus. If they could truly and singularly focus on the programs they're trying to develop, especially for Metronome, they could get a lot accomplished.

Each takes his or her turn adding to this discussion about focus, but it's Kate's insight that catches KC's attention.

"You know how you're never halfway done with a project by the deadline's halfway mark?" she begins. Not everyone understands what she means, so she tries to reframe her point. "What I mean is, if you have three weeks to study for a test, you're almost never half finished with your studying at the one-and-a-half-week mark. But the more you focus on it, the more immersed you become in it, and the more things just start to flow. And so if you've really been focusing, by the last week, you're able to complete a ton! Added to that, there's the positive sense of accomplishment that comes from making progress. That can motivate you even further. It really lets you extend your reach. In the past, when we were able to stay one hundred percent focused on just one project, it was amazing; we'd often surpass our goals."

There's an audible silence when Kate finishes. KC looks around at the others and sees engaged, hopeful faces. *These are highly motivated individuals who just want to do their jobs well—not unlike the basketball players back in Edmonton,* he thinks to himself.

"So what gets in the way of that focus?" Karen asks. "What's preventing you from being able to focus?"

As soon as she gets these words out, everyone starts talking at once.

"Oh, there are new distractions every day."

"A hundred different demands."

"One department or another needs our IT expertise."

"It's not like these are all frivolous or irrelevant distractions," says Dominic. "Often, a whole group in another department is held up because they need our expertise to get them over a hurdle. So what can we do? We have to help them out."

KC listens as they describe these distractions and even defend them. When it's his turn to speak, he draws from his recent experience at the training camp. "I've been working with the women's national basketball team. With them, sometimes as pressure increases during a game and things start falling apart, one player will take it upon herself to try to solve the problem. But it's not a problem that an individual player can solve. The whole team needs to adjust as a unit."

"That's exactly what's happening here," Kate says. "At least a version of that. A few weeks ago, some people started coming in early to try to advance the project on their own. Others stayed late and worked on it. The problem was that then they had to bring everyone up to speed on what they'd been doing. That took a lot of time."

"And it created some tension," adds Lucas. "Henri, who was the first to try to go it alone, created some real havoc."

At the mention of Henri, KC notices a perceptible shift in the atmosphere in the room. Karen must notice it too, because she's quick to steer the conversation away from that particular topic.

"Okay, let's review," she says. "We're making progress here. We've identified that the Metronome project requires focus. There needs to be some dedicated time for this project, time that allows everyone to focus on this and only this. It's also clear that there are demands from other departments that need to be tended to. I think in the next session two days from now, we need to figure out how we can meet both of these needs—and stay sane."

"Good luck to us with that!" says Kate.

Lucas turns and looks straight at KC. "Kenneth, do you think it's possible?" he asks.

KC doesn't bat an eye. "Of course I do. You've got a lot of great things working here. You're a motivated group. You all want to do your best. I'm sure we can come up with a plan that will help you to do exactly that."

Lucas sinks a little into his chair and says, "I hope you're right. For the most part, this is a pretty terrific group, although we do have one major distractor."

There's no need for him to identify the culprit. Everyone in the room nods his or her acknowledgement. Everyone thinks about Henri.

After the meeting, KC and Karen sit down by themselves to hammer out the details for the upcoming workshop. Once they've come up with a solid plan, KC collects his things to go, but before he does, he pumps Karen for a little more information about Douglas. KC is curious about the guy he met briefly that morning.

"You're asking me about his personality? His temperament?" she asks in order to clarify.

"I guess I am," KC says hesitantly. "He's obviously a very intelligent man. And people like him. But it's true that he can be a bit disruptive. What's that about?"

Karen pauses to think over his question. Then she says, "Douglas is a bit of a visionary. He's an ideas man. But there aren't nearly enough hours in the day for him, or for any of us, to carry out all the ideas that pass through his head. Having said that, he's also very practical. If you can make a solid case for something, he'll easily change or modify his position. He loves concrete evidence. He's also very likeable, as I'm sure you saw yourself."

"Would it be out of place for me to send him a book and a few articles related to energy management? Just the sort of stuff we're introducing to Dominic's team?"

"What did you have in mind exactly? Do you mind telling me?" she asks.

"Not at all. It's just that there's this terrific book called *Choke* I'd like to send him. The author, Dr. Sian Beilock, uses a lot of golfing examples to reinforce what we're teaching. So I figured with Douglas's obvious passion for the game, well, I thought he might enjoy it."

"Oh. So this would be purely for his enjoyment?" Karen says, and she laughs. "Thank goodness. I thought maybe you were trying to manipulate him a little—trying to win him over."

"I might be doing a little bit of that, too. But I'm surprised you'd object to it!" KC says.

"Heck no!" Karen exclaims. "I'm all for manipulation—as long as it's done with the best intentions. And the best intentions, of course, mean that I'm well served!"

"Of course."

"You mentioned an article? What's it about?"

"It's on the myth of multitasking. I thought it might be a good read for him, considering how much stuff he piles on you and on the others. There's a particularly good article I'm thinking of, backed by some sound research that makes it very clear there's actually no such thing as multitasking."

"No such thing as multitasking? That's crazy. I multitask all the time," she says. To demonstrate her point, she picks up a few pencils and juggles them handily as she continues her conversation with him. "Look, I'm multitasking right now! I'm juggling pencils. I'm talking to you. I'm discussing ways to solve our company's problems." She's hardly able to get these sentences out before she loses track of the pencils and watches them fall one after another to the floor.

"Certainly it exists in the sense of doing a couple things simultaneously. But it's very clear that you can only focus on one thing at a time." KC picks one of the pencils up off of the floor and lays it on the table in front of her. "Multitasking involves shifting your attention from one thing to another thing. Not only does the shifting take time, but you've also got to factor in the time required to refamiliarize yourself with the task you've shifted to. Now, if one of the tasks that you're doing is brainless, in the sense that it can be done without thought, then—and only then—could you really multitask."

"And a brainless task would be?" she asks.

"Something that's so well ingrained that you're unconsciously competent at it. In my world, I can't think of many things where I could effectively multitask. Maybe if I was stuffing envelopes or something, I could also pay attention to what you were talking to me about. But maybe not! Even that simple task might distract me, and I'd miss things you were saying."

Karen lets a mischievous look pass over her face. "As a woman with three children, I can think of millions of things I do simultaneously."

KC knows better than to get into an argument with a mother about her ability to juggle a million tasks at once. It's a dangerous conversation, and he feels slightly on edge, but he knows that his point about multitasking is apt—and important. "I'm not going down that rabbit hole, Karen. The fact of the matter is that workplace multitasking is, by and large, a myth."

"I agree. I agree, but that was a good opportunity to get your defensiveness riled up. I couldn't pass on it."

"I am not defensive," KC says defensively before easing into a smile.

The next day, on his way to his morning workout at the gym, KC drops off the book and article in Douglas's office. Douglas isn't there, but once again, the office door is open, so KC lets himself in. He leaves the reading material on his desk, along with a polite note, and then he takes a few minutes to look around. You can learn a lot about someone by looking at his or her workspace.

The first thing that strikes him is the orderliness of the office. It's also personalized. There are a lot of reminders of Douglas's personal life, his out-of-the-office life, including photographs of his family and some from his college days and a wall dedicated to what must have been social events connected with Optimal IT. KC is about to take a closer look at these photographs, when he hears a noise in the hall and decides it's time for him to leave.

The following morning, while he checks his e-mail in advance of the team workshop, KC is surprised to find a message from Douglas. He opens up the e-mail, which reads,

> Kenneth,
> Thanks for the reading material. Haven't had time to read the whole *Choke* book yet, but I like what I've read so far. And I took a look at this article on multitasking. Not bad, not bad. I see the logic in it, Kenneth. Might be something worth considering in terms of my own work. Particularly loved the three quotes below. Thought it might apply to my staff, seeing as they all have what the author, Sian Beilock, calls horsepower.

Taking a step back rather than running full steam ahead when you have a task that requires a heavy dose of working-memory can be the key to completing it successfully.

Glucose, which is the primary source of energy for the body's cells including brain cells, becomes depleted when you continuously exert effort on a difficult thinking and reasoning task. If you don't take time to recoup your resources, your performance on whatever you do next can suffer.

Even though you might feel as if you don't have the luxury of catching your breath, going down the wrong solution path, or operating with all "glucose cylinders on empty" is a worse option—especially for those people who have the most cognitive horsepower and the most potential to begin with.

Golf game soon?
DA

"Jeez," KC says to himself. "I just gave him that article yesterday, and already he's trying to put it into practice."

KC rereads the e-mail, drafts a quick response and then gets ready to head over to the workshop site—the hotel near Optimal IT—for today's workshop with the team.

When he arrives at the hotel, he's eager to show Karen the e-mail. She, of course, is thrilled with Douglas's response.

"Oh, terrific! I'm glad we're getting him on board," she says.

"As much as I'm delighted at how quickly he integrates and applies what he reads, I have to ask: Does this man ever sleep? I mean, I just dropped this stuff off yesterday, not even twenty-four hours ago, and he's read the whole article and parts of the book."

"Well, he's a multitasker, so he probably read them both at once," she jokes.

"Which would mean he read neither of them carefully."

"But seriously, Douglas is pretty incredible. He's got that cognitive horsepower. He sees application almost instantly. That's one of his strengths. As for how he finds the time, I know his wife is out of town visiting grandchildren, so he's batching it up right now. He probably spent the whole evening on what you gave him."

"No kidding."

Their conversation is broken up by the arrival of the others, who all quickly take their seats, eager to get started, make progress and find ways to make their work lives easier.

Karen begins the workshop by asking the same question she asked the three programmers a couple of days prior. "What's the one thing you could change that would really make a difference?"

The collective answers of the group are in line with what the three programmers said: there's an attention problem, a focus problem. Everyone agrees.

From here, the workshop gallops along nicely. KC takes the reins and leads the group through a series of interactive sessions, the end result of which is the team coming up with a plan they believe will help them address their main area of concern: their ability to focus on the Metronome project and to continue supporting the other departments.

The plan is as follows. The group decides—with Henri serving as the lone voice of dissension—that they have the most cognitive horsepower early in the day, when they first arrive at work. Therefore, that's when they'll focus on Metronome. They agree to take a 15-minute break at the 90-minute mark. After the break, they'll commit another 90 minutes exclusively to Metronome.

They also agree to take 15 minutes each over the course of the morning to respond to requests from other departments. These responses are to follow a strict formula. If the issue the department has raised is something they can cover within 15 minutes, they will see to it. If not, they'll let the department know that they won't be dealing with that issue until one o'clock, when they shift their focus away from Metronome.

Finally, in the last 10 minutes of the morning, they will identify three things that went well that day and one thing that could use improvement—something they can focus on the following day.

Although most of the team agrees to this new breakdown of work hours, there is one loud objection.

"Why would we waste ten minutes talking about that nonsense, when we could use that time to get more work done?" Henri asks.

Lucas says, "I wouldn't say we're wasting those minutes. We're just—"

Henri quickly cuts him off. He continues to raise his objections, his voice booming over Lucas's. "I also don't see why we need that fifteen-minute break in the morning. There's no need to talk to the other departments about their issues. I mean, honestly, they leave us hanging all the time. If they can't help us out, why should we bother getting back to them? I say we just give them a little taste of their own medicine."

A pall descends over the group for a moment. The positive momentum built up over the last hour seems on the verge of being undone. But then Kate leans forward in her chair, looks right at Henri and, in a firm voice, says, "If you don't know the answer to those questions, Henri, you can't have been paying any attention. The review at the end of the morning is supposed to function as a reward to energize us for all we've done. As for not responding to the others, for most of us, that would hang over us like a black cloud. It would just be an energy drain. It would keep us from being properly engaged the rest of the morning."

Henri doesn't bother with a retort. He crosses his arms and shakes his head slightly. The tension in the room remains, but KC is pleased—and relieved—to hear Kate speak up like this, standing up for herself and for the group.

"We've got a plan here—a good, solid plan," says Kate.

"I agree. I think it could work," adds Dominic.

A chorus of agreement follows, each member of the team affirming the work they've done so far. As each member expresses support and enthusiasm for the plan they've come up with, the tension begins to abate. It's almost as though the group is collectively trying to shed the blanket of Henri's negativity with a reaffirmation of the plan.

Their efforts seem to work. When the workshop ends a few minutes later, KC notes that a lighter mood has been restored to the room. As the participants gather their things and begin to leave, he sees relaxed postures and easy smiles. Even Dominic, who typically projects a twitchy, slightly frazzled sort of energy, seems a little more relaxed than he did the first day KC met him.

"That went well, eh?" Karen says.

"Sure. I think we're on track."

"Maybe we could meet up for a quick debrief tomorrow?" she says.

"Sorry, Karen. If you want to hear my voice tomorrow, you'll have to turn on your radio."

A small crease of puzzlement appears between her eyebrows. "You're back on the radio? When I heard you a few weeks ago, I thought you were just doing a guest spot to promote your book."

"I was. But things have snowballed. Now I'm moonlighting as a radio host."

Karen slaps his arm playfully. "Kenneth! You've been holding out on me. Why didn't you tell me?"

"To be perfectly honest, the whole thing has me a little nervous."

"I didn't know you got nervous. Doesn't seem like you."

"Happens to the best of us."

"Don't you have tricks for that? Some tips for managing nervous energy?"

"Sure, I've got some good techniques. But still, it's new ground for me. New ground always induces nerves."

"Nonsense, Kenneth. You're a terrific speaker. You're great on air; you've got the perfect voice for radio."

"And the face for it too!" he jokes.

"Oh, come off it, Kenneth. Now you're just fishing for compliments."

"I am," he concedes. "But you know, a few well-timed compliments can really help settle someone's nerves."

Karen laughs as they pack up the last of their things and head out.

CHAPTER 8

LET THE SHOW BEGIN

In this chapter, KC talks about the key skill of energizing and encourages listeners to take "smoke" breaks and to act abnormally. We also learn of the overloaded life of the last caller, Farhan.

KC arrives at the radio station with a swirl of nerves in his belly. He sees Bill through the glass panels surrounding the studio and gives him a quick wave but makes a detour to the washroom before joining him. Sometimes washrooms seem like the few remaining sanctuaries in the world. Before a big presentation, KC often retreats to this particular refuge. He likes to stand in front of the mirror, straighten his tie, look himself in the eye and check his energy level.

Today, as he performs this ritual, he manages to shake off his nerves a little by reminding himself that he's not alone; Bill is there to help him host the show. *Just have fun,* he thinks. *This is new ground, and new ground brings with it new energy.*

Joining Bill in the studio, KC takes his seat at the U-shaped table. The show—or at least the portion of the show that KC is hosting—is scheduled to run from five o'clock to six o'clock. However, that hour-long designation isn't strictly accurate. The truth is, news, sports, weather and traffic reports eat up the first eight minutes of the hour. Then comes a break for commercials, followed by a few minutes for introductory remarks. It's almost ten after five by the time KC and Bill get the chance to delve into the topic of the day: energizing.

"So, Kenneth, you're going to be with us once a month for the next little while," Bill begins. His tone is easy and confident—it's clear he's an old hand at the radio game. "I know there are a lot of aspects of energy management you want to cover, but today we're focusing on energizing. Is that right?"

"That's right. How to boost your energy. Your energy level has a huge effect on your performance level. It's hard to perform at a high level when you're feeling flat or lacking motivation. We all know this feeling. We all have moments like this every day." As KC speaks, he feels himself settling into this new role. He becomes more relaxed, and his nerves calm down. He's able to enjoy himself.

"I'm definitely guilty of feeling flat," Bill says. "I often feel that way in the third hour of the show. I don't know why it happens, but my energy just starts to tank."

"Like I said, that happens to everyone. But these drops in energy can be especially problematic when we make our livings interacting with others."

"Why is that?" Bill asks, looking mildly worried.

"Because often, people misread our listlessness, our low energy, as disinterest. They can take it personally."

Bill screws his face into an embarrassed grimace. "Yikes. That's sure not what I want to be projecting. Jeez, I feel like I should be apologizing to everyone who's ever been around me in the third hour of the show. Sorry, gang. Sorry, faithful listeners. I'm interested! I'm interested—I swear! I'm just having energy management problems."

KC allows a chuckle at Bill's theatrics before he gets back into his discussion on energizing. He explains that each person has an optimal level of energy for a given task, factoring in the degree of difficulty involved and the person's skill level. Energizing is particularly important when the task is one that's been performed a hundred times before. When something is incredibly familiar, almost rote, it's easy not to be totally engaged in it.

"This is when we underperform, when we make errors," KC explains.

"It would also open the door for distractions, wouldn't it?"

"Yes, absolutely. We can be distracted by our environment, by our thoughts. We notice our own boredom. The task really starts to drag. And so there's just no sense of satisfaction."

"So why does this happen?" Bill asks. "Why the energy drop?"

"Oh, there are dozens of reasons for low energy. You might not be getting adequate rest. Poor diet and a lack of exercise can have catastrophic effects on your energy level. Or you might be draining your energy with worrying or negative thinking. The body sends us very real messages about our energy levels, and those messages should be listened to. I want to focus on situations where you can energize—but never at the expense of overriding those messages."

"Okay," Bill says with a nod at the clock. "I think we're off to a great start here. Right now, we're going to head into a quick commercial break, and when we come back, Kenneth and I will be taking some of your calls."

KC can hardly believe they've already been at it for 10 minutes. While the commercials roll, he says, "Boy, time really flies on the radio, huh?"

"It does sometimes, yeah. It sure helps when there's activity on the switchboards. Take a look at this, Kenneth. We're all lit up."

KC looks at the computer screen that tracks listener feedback. It's a constant stream of movement as more and more feedback pops up. In fewer than 10 minutes, he's managed to generate a solid response from the show's listeners.

When the commercials near their end, Bill pulls the mic toward him, readying himself for the next segment. He says, "Welcome back. If you're just tuning in, I've got Kenneth Coghill cohosting the first hour of the *Drive Home Show* with me today. And right now, he's taking your calls. So let's see here." Bill pauses for half a second while he selects a caller. "Hi, Mona. You're on the air."

"Oh, hello," says a young but tired voice. From those two simple words, it's clear this woman has had a long day. "Yeah, I just wanted to say that this energy stuff really hits home for me. I always start my day with a ton of energy. But by midafternoon, I just feel like I'm sucking air, you know? So I end up drinking a million cups of coffee or Red Bull or Diet Coke. Or all three."

KC sits forward in his chair. He wants to know more about the caller and the details of her day. "Tell me a little about your mornings. How productive are you?"

"Well, let's see. I usually arrive at work early and push through right to lunch without much of an issue. Right after lunch, my energy is still okay. But then it just starts to fall apart. The last few hours of the day feel like a grinding marathon."

KC smiles to himself, reflecting on the familiarity of this problem. "A lot of people view their days as marathons. But the fact is, we human beings aren't designed for marathons. We're much better sprinters."

"What does that mean exactly?" Mona asks. "Should I shorten my work days to just a few hours? I'm not sure my boss will go for that," she adds with a laugh.

"No, I imagine he won't. What I'm talking about is breaking up our days into smaller, bite-size pieces. Work hard—sprint—for ninety minutes or so. Then take a break. Breaks are especially important in the morning hours. They help ensure that there's still water in the well, that there's a store of energy to pull from by the end of the day."

"Sometimes in the afternoons, I take minibreaks," Mona says. "I'll get up from my desk for a few minutes or maybe have a quick chat with a friend."

"Those are definitely great things to do, Mona. Those activities can give you a shot of energy. Unfortunately, they won't be much use if you're already completely worn out. The idea here is that you can't wait until your energy is fully drained before you try to refill the supply. Let me ask you this. Would it be possible to get outside during the morning, to take a quick outdoor break?"

There's a pause on the line while Mona considers the suggestion. When she responds, she's hesitant. "Hmm, well, I mean, I guess I could—technically. But to be honest, it'd feel pretty strange to just get up and go outside. Especially when there's lots of work I should be doing at my desk."

This is the response KC expected. People don't want to be seen abandoning their posts, so they all stay in position at their desks, even when their productivity levels are tanking.

"Have you ever smoked, Mona?" he asks.

"Ugh. No. Hate the habit," she says.

"I'm going to make an odd recommendation."

"As long as it's not to pick up smoking."

"Well, it is! Sort of. I want you take up the habit of smoking. But without actually smoking."

"Um, I don't get it."

"Smokers have no problem getting outside for their breaks. When they need smoke breaks, they just take them. I want you to do the same. I want you to take a break and head outside. Only skip the smoking part. Just take a walk instead. Or sit. Or think."

"Huh."

KC can hear from the tone of her voice that she isn't convinced by the idea. "Let me tell you a story that'll help get the idea across," he says.

"Okay," says Mona.

"Oh, I love story time," says Bill, shifting in his chair to get comfortable.

"I'm so glad to hear that. Because when you've lived as long as I have, the stories really start to pile up. This particular story is from my university days."

"A story from the 1920s?" Bill jokes.

"I'm not quite that old, Bill. Not quite. No, my old school days were in the sixties. And back then, I worked summers underground in a mine."

"In a mine? Wow," Bill says, now fully interested in the story. His expression is curious and attentive. He has laid aside all joking for the moment.

KC's story begins in his first year at the mines. He worked with a man named Emile. KC and Emile were what were called nippers. They moved from level to level throughout the mine, cleaning what needed to be cleaned. Every so often, Emile would stop what they were doing and say, "All right, Ken. Smoke break."

Neither of them smoked, but that never stopped Emile from calling the smoke break.

Emile explained it to him like this: "Eight months of the year, I don't work with a summer student like you. And in those eight months, I get a lot more breaks—just because the guy I normally work with is a smoker. I realized that smokers get a lot more breaks than those of us who don't smoke. Didn't seem fair. So I decided to take smoke breaks anyway. Smoke-free smoke breaks."

KC smiles as he recounts this story to Mona. Those were good summers.

"Smoke-free smoke breaks," she repeats. "I could try that."

"I don't mean you have to go downstairs and hang out with the smokers. But there's something very energizing about being outside, even for just a few minutes."

Once again, there's a short pause on the line. But this time, when Mona begins to speak, her voice is livelier and more hopeful. "You know, there's this nice little park near my office. I used to go for walks there during my lunch hour. Now that I think back on it, I did have a lot more energy when I was doing that. I can't think why I stopped—probably because I didn't think I had time for it. That park might be a nice place to visit on my smoke-free smoke break."

"Sounds perfect," KC says.

He's just started to get the ball rolling with Mona when Bill interjects. "Sure does. Some good advice from our guest host," Bill says. He motions to the clock again for KC's benefit while quickly but skillfully ending the conversation with Mona and sending the show into another commercial break.

There's a lot more KC could have discussed with Mona, but given the time constraints, he's satisfied with the discussion. It's a starting point. From every starting point, there's a progression. If people are learning to dive into water, they start on one knee on the deck of the pool, not on the 10-metre diving tower. If they start at the right place in the progression, people naturally move on to the next step. When people fail to make changes, it's often because they bite off more than they can chew. They try to change too much at once. A smoke break is a manageable change. It's a good starting point.

This time during the commercial break, KC takes a moment to sip some water and relax. "You know," he says to Bill, "these commercials are great built-in energy management breaks for you."

"I guess that's true. I should find ways to make better use of them. Maybe even some stretching? I get so stiff sitting in this chair for hours on end."

"That's an idea."

"Yeah, it is, isn't it?" Bill says as he rolls his head to the left and to the right. But this attempt at getting in a quick stretch is cut short. The break is already almost over. "Let's pick this up again later, Kenneth. Right now, we're back on the air."

The next call they take comes from Kristen, a synchronized swimmer. KC is thrilled to have an athlete call in—and a swimmer at that. He's been to three Olympics with the synchronized-swimming team, and he knows the incredible demands of the sport. Most viewers of the sport only see the nose clips and the forced smiles. They understand little about the difficulty of the sport. At the Atlanta games, KC read an article listing the five toughest sports in the Olympics, and synchronized swimming was on that list.

"What's on your mind, Kristen?" he asks.

"Well, I'm hoping to make the national team this year, but the training load is so gruelling. It's just so rough. I guess I'm having trouble keeping up the energy for it all."

"What you have to remember, Kristen, is that what you're trying to do is abnormal."

"Uh, okay."

"It's not normal to try to make a national team. Most people aren't doing that."

"No, I guess they aren't."

"So if we're agreed that what you're trying to do is abnormal, you have to be willing to act abnormally. A cancer patient once told me that dealing with cancer wasn't normal. So she had to upgrade her optimism. Because she was dealing with an abnormal situation, normal, everyday optimism wouldn't do."

"Huh. I'm not sure I entirely understand."

KC decides to operationalize the concept. He comes at it from a way she might be more familiar with. "What's the toughest drill you do in practice?"

"Oh, no question. The eggbeater."

"Ah, the infamous eggbeater." KC knows the drill, and he knows how much swimmers hate it. In this drill, the swimmer does lengths of the pool with her arms above her head and her legs rotating around like eggbeaters underwater. At the Olympic level, the practice is to keep the bellybutton dry. It's a killer. "What are your teammates' reactions when the coach tells them the eggbeater is next?"

"Ha! A lot of groans and moans. Some *Oh Gods*. Everyone hates it."

"Is that a normal reaction?" he asks.

"Yes. Definitely. The eggbeater is terrible."

"Right. It seems like the abnormal reaction to that drill would be total enthusiasm—someone shouting, 'Let's go! We can do this!'"

"I guess that's true."

"But a moment ago, we agreed that you're trying to do something abnormal—to make the national team and go to the Olympics. So sometimes you need to have an abnormal reaction to things. You need to find abnormal enthusiasm. Maybe you can be the one who pumps up the energy for the group, the one who shouts, 'Let's do it!'"

Kristen is quick to respond. "I've done that. I really have! But I got tired of trying to motivate nine other swimmers."

"Sure, that's understandable. Being the constant source of energy is exhausting. But let me ask you this: Would your teammates be interested in boosting their energy levels and having more-upbeat practices?"

"Oh yeah, no question about that. It's something we discuss all the time. But we don't ever do anything about it."

KC nods to himself. He faced a similar situation with the synchronized-swimming team ahead of the Sydney Olympics. Although a lot of the swimmers could generate enthusiasm and energy, no one wanted to take on the role of full-time cheerleader.

"I used a simple process with the synchro team years ago. I

paired up ten swimmers and assigned each pair a weekday. On their appointed day, the pair was responsible for energizing the team and keeping things upbeat. The pair was also allotted fifteen minutes of practice to bring some fun and energy to things. They could use that time however they wanted, and believe me, they got pretty creative sometimes."

"That does sound like fun," Kristen says.

"Oh, it really was. And it worked wonderfully. There was a lot less anxiety around the practices. Could your team do that?"

"Hey, yeah, that's a great idea. Thanks, Kenneth."

"Thanks for calling."

As soon as the conversation with Kristen wraps up, Bill throws to another commercial break. This time, during the break, Bill gets out of his chair and does some easy stretches. With his arms over his head, he tilts his gaze to KC. "It's going really well, Ken. Looks like we're deluged with calls here. How about we take one more caller after the break and then wind things down with a promo for the next show? Sound good?"

"Sure. Good plan."

But as happens with many great plans, this one doesn't come to pass, because the next caller, the last caller, throws a wrench into things. The next caller is Farhan.

"Hello, Farhan. Glad to have you with us," Bill says.

"Hi. Hello. Hi," he stammers.

The caller seems nervous or uncomfortable about being live on air, so KC tries to ease him along. "What's going on, Farhan? What prompted you to call?"

"Well, um, this is the first time I've ever called in. But I listen to the show a lot. Actually, well, I'm sort of surprised that I've called in. It's really not like me."

"Oh no? So what caused this un-like-you behaviour?"

There's a strained silence on the line before Farhan begins to speak again. "I guess I had a bit of a wake-up call last week. You see—I work in a government ministry, and I've recently been promoted."

Farhan goes on to explain the circumstances around his

promotion to a leadership position. At first, he was excited about the promotion, but as time has gone on, he's realized that the workload is significantly greater than he expected. He still has to perform all of the duties associated with his previous job, but now he has the added responsibility of supervising others.

"I've always seen myself in this sort of leadership role. But now that I'm in one, I think it's a much-bigger mandate than I imagined."

With hardly a pause in his speech, Farhan describes how little control he has at the government job. Everything seems last-minute, and things can suddenly take a sharp turn based on the whim of an elected official. The information pours out of him. Calling in to a radio show might be new behaviour for Farhan, but now that he's done it, he seems to have taken to it.

"Sounds like you're dealing with a lot, Farhan," KC says.

"Oh, that's not the half of it. Then there's my family. The job is also having a huge effect on my family." With that, Farhan sets off on a discussion of his family situation. He has a wife and two kids—a 13-year-old son and a 4-year-old daughter, the latter of whom was, as he puts it, a "wonderful accident." Having that second child has complicated things.

No kidding, thinks KC. His own son-in-law once said, shortly after the birth of a second child, that the first child was a great hobby, but two … Well, his son-in-law never did finish that sentence.

Farhan continues speaking, finding more angles to the situation and more to talk about. But it's almost the top of the hour, and time is running low. Every few seconds, Bill looks anxiously at the clock. KC's eye, however, is drawn to the switchboard, which is lit up like a Christmas tree. Farhan's frank and open discussion of his problems must be resonating with listeners.

When Farhan at last allows a pause in his monologue, KC jumps in to try to steer the conversation. "You mentioned a wake-up call, Farhan. Tell me about that."

Farhan doesn't need more of a prompt than this. Within seconds, he's back at it, describing a scene from a week earlier: his son's soccer game. Farhan was swamped with work and forgot about the game until the last minute, so he arrived very late.

On the drive home after the game, his son was quiet, almost despondent. Farhan tried to spark a conversation, but the boy would have nothing of it. They passed the evening in relative silence. Later that night, Farhan's wife raised the issue of the forgotten soccer game again. She wanted to know how he could've forgotten about the game, how he could've been late. Farhan didn't have a good answer for her. He didn't know how he could've forgotten about it. He and his wife were constantly juggling schedules, trying to figure out who was doing what with which of their children. Sometimes wires got crossed.

"I told my wife I don't know how I forgot. It just slipped through the cracks. But then she told me that when she went to say good night to our boy, she asked him if my being late had bothered him. And you know what he said?"

"What did he say, Farhan?"

"He said, 'Even when Dad's there, he's not really there.' That's what he said. My wife asked him what he meant by that, and he said that I often have my head down, that I'm always looking at my iPhone, always texting. I'm not paying enough attention. And I had no idea he felt that way. That was a real wake-up call."

KC leans toward his mic to respond, but before he gets a word out, Farhan's voice picks up again. This time, his words are imbued with a deep, raw emotion.

"But you know—I was so mad when she told me that. It's really hard for me to make it to those soccer games. I try very hard. Honestly, I do. So I was mad that my life doesn't allow me to really be where I am in the moment. Mostly, I was mad because he was right. I want to be a great father, a great husband, and a terrific manager. I want to be good at my job. How do I do all those things?"

Silence hangs in the air after this impassioned plea. Even Bill is caught up in the moment. KC takes a deep breath. Then he says, "Farhan, you've raised a dozen important issues here, and I want to talk about all of them. But unfortunately we're out of time here. Would you consider leaving your contact information with our producer? We can talk about this off air."

"Yes," he says quietly. The word comes out as a squeak.

CHAPTER 9

 **FARHAN**

In this chapter, Kenneth meets with Farhan in a park, and they devise a one-thing plan.

On the drive home from the radio station, KC can't help but replay his conversations with each of the three callers.

"If only I'd had more time!" he says to himself. "There's so much more I could've shared with them."

With the first caller, he could have mentioned that breaks are beneficial not only for productivity but also for creativity. He could have stressed that the effectiveness of a break depends more on the level of disengagement from the task than on the length of the break. It's also vital to consider the company you keep during a break. A break partner can play a huge role in the quality of disengagement. You can take a break with an incredibly negative person—someone who spends the entire break complaining about work—and wind up feeling even worse than before.

"I really wish I'd mentioned all that," KC mumbles in his car. "I hope Mona doesn't spoil her breaks in the park by taking them with the wrong coworker."

KC often thinks of people as either friends or accomplices. Some people encourage you in ways that are good for you. These are friends. But others, the accomplices, lead you down a path of discontentment. The conductor of the Boston Philharmonic, Ben Zander, once described interaction with an accomplice as "the conversation of no possibilities."

For about half the drive home, KC frets over this first caller and the myriad of things he neglected to mention to her. During the second half of the drive, his mind turns to Kristen, the synchronized swimmer. He comes up with a whole new list of stories and ideas he missed out on communicating to her. His mind is so preoccupied with all he might have said that it doesn't have the opportunity to register frustration about the traffic he's stuck in this afternoon.

Thinking over his conversation with Kristen, KC recalls a company he once worked with in Seattle. This company energized its workforce during a tough transitional time by borrowing a wonderful tradition from Mexican culture. In this tradition—translated as "secret admirer"—all of the employees drop file cards into a large drum on their way out of the office on Friday. On the front of the cards, they write their names and their departments, and on the back, they write three things they enjoy. Any three things—whatever tickles them.

The following Monday morning, each person selects a card from the drum and becomes the so-called secret admirer of the person whose card he or she chooses. The secret admirer has a two-dollar budget to provide the admired party with the three things—or some interpretation of the three things—written on the card. Given this limited budget, the exercise requires tremendous creativity. At the company in Seattle, most people demonstrated that they were up to the task.

One day around noon, KC was sitting in the company's lunchroom. A woman approached his table, where he sitting with three of the company's employees. All of them were enjoying sandwiches on nice crusty bread.

"See that guy in the plaid shirt over there?" she said.

They all looked to see whom she was pointing at and then nodded in unison.

"Well, I'm his secret admirer," she continued. "His card says that he likes travel and music. So I've got a good plan."

"I like a good plan," said KC.

"Will you four walk over there, pick up his chair and carry him around the lunchroom? And maybe sing a song to him while you're doing it? When you put him down, tell him the song and trip are from his secret admirer."

KC was never one to say no to such fun. The others jumped at the chance as well. They strolled up to the unsuspecting man, who was quietly eating his lunch, and they hoisted him up into the air, carried him around the lunchroom and belted out an old Johnny Cash tune while they did it.

What energy that simple act brought to the lunchroom! And there were hundreds of these energizing moments throughout the week the company ran the event. Even as he thinks of it now, KC chuckles at the fun they had. Without KC realizing it, the memory prompts him to hum a few bars of the Johnny Cash number they sang that day.

He's still humming that song when he pulls into his driveway a few minutes later. As he eases the car into the garage, his mind finally arrives at Farhan. Farhan's issues are many and complicated, and KC isn't sure where to start. He remains seated in his parked car, lost in thought, wondering how to untangle the knot of issues Farhan raised. What's the best approach with him? What's the most effective starting point? Before he decides on any particular course, he knows he'll have to hear more from the man himself.

The next morning, after a long run under cool, cloudy skies, KC sits down at his computer. He hasn't been able to stop thinking about Farhan and his troubles. The first thing he does is retrieve Farhan's contact information, which he collected from the show's producers yesterday before he left the radio station. He shoots Farhan an e-mail, offering to meet up, telling him the sooner, the better.

Within an hour, he gets a reply. After a few back-and-forth e-mails, they arrange to meet at a park near enough to both Farhan's office and KC's home. They're both juggling busy schedules, so it's a relief to find a place that works well on both ends.

As soon as KC arrives at the park, he realizes he has no idea what Farhan looks like. The realization surprises him. Whether aware of it or not, when we hear someone's voice, we immediately paint a picture in our minds of what this person must look like. But often, that picture is inaccurate. Today's example proves no exception. KC finds himself expecting someone small in stature, lanky maybe, but the man who approaches him is about six foot two and has a thick frame. He looks to be in good shape.

"Kenneth?" the man says. "I'm Farhan."

"Oh, hi there. Good to meet you," KC says, and he rises to shake Farhan's hand. "What do you say to a walk?"

"Sure."

The clouds from earlier that morning have started to thin, and it's shaping up to be a pleasant afternoon with great weather for a walk in the park. They walk along the paved paths, spending their first few minutes making small talk, getting to know each other. When Farhan seems relaxed enough, KC broaches the reason for their meeting.

"Your call really stayed with me," he says.

"Oh, well, yes. I think I was feeling a bit overwhelmed at the time," Farhan says, trying to downplay the issues. At first, he seems slightly embarrassed about his spontaneous confession from the day before. However, it's not long before he makes it clear that his feeling of being overwhelmed wasn't an isolated moment. It's a chronic feeling—one that needs urgent attention.

"I'm beginning to feel like a failure," Farhan says.

"How so?"

"I'm letting my son down. I'm not managing people as well as I'd like to. My home life—well, it needs improvement."

"Often, failure is a critical part of the change process. Framing your wake-up call as a failure instead of as an opportunity to grow isn't helping you. It's sucking energy right out of you. Falling down is just part of the learning process."

"I must be learning a lot then," Farhan says, his tone still thoroughly dejected.

KC slows his stride so that he can take a good look at Farhan, whose dissatisfaction is etched on his face. "The good news is that you're disappointed with yourself," KC says.

"That's good news? How is that good news?" Farhan asks, stopping dead in his tracks.

KC claps his back and chuckles. He motions for Farhan to carry on with their walk, and once they're back at it, he says, "My mentor, a psychologist named Kazimierz Dabrowski, said that mentally healthy individuals were blessed with the gift of internal crisis, which is inherent within the painful journey of human development."

Farhan stares at him with blank eyes. "Translate that for me, Kenneth."

"Feelings and emotions are tragic gifts."

"How is something both tragic and a gift?"

"They're tragic in the sense that dealing with them is difficult. But they're gifts in the sense that they help us move forward. What you have to do is figure out what you're going to do with all the energy underneath your disappointment. Where are you going to put that energy?"

"What do you mean?"

"You can use it to energize and move yourself forward along a different path, or you can direct it inward and continue to feel down about yourself. You know, it's a funny thing, but sometimes it isn't until we're colossally upset about something that we decide to change it. I think that's exactly the point you're at right now."

"I definitely don't want to carry on doing what I've been doing, if that's what you're saying."

"That's exactly what I'm saying, Farhan. So let me ask you this: What is the one thing that you could do differently that would really change things for you?"

"Hm. One thing, huh?"

"Just one thing."

Farhan has trouble answering the question. He throws out a lot of ideas for things he'd like to change, but he has trouble narrowing his focus to just one thing. It takes a few minutes and a few hundred more metres of path before he finally says, "I need to figure out how to feel less drained all the time."

From the difficulty Farhan has in limiting his focus to arrive at this central goal, it's clear to KC that part of the problem is a sort of mental sprawl. Farhan is trying to undertake too much at once.

In their book *Switch*, Dan and Chip Heath discuss how you can find motivation by shrinking down the mission. Big changes come from a succession of small changes. In KC's own work with athletes, this lesson is something he constantly works on. It's crucial to keep the athletes focused on small performance goals as they make their way to larger end goals. The process is like building a staircase. The landing at the top is the end goal, but as you're building the staircase, you've got to focus on the step you're on. The successful completion of each step generates the energy to keep going and work your way up to the landing at the top.

Farhan's end goal is to feel less drained, so they need to figure out how to keep moving him toward that goal. First and foremost, they need to identify the next step.

"Let's pick a place to start. What do you think is contributing most to your energy drain?" KC asks.

"Hm, well, let me think. I guess I'd say it's my management practice. That needs the most work. The more I think about it, the more I realize that I'm not getting energy out of my work at all. And it's funny, because I always thought I would. Being a manager, a leader, is something I really wanted to be. I wish it was making me happier."

"Okay, let's talk about that. What could you accomplish as a manager that might make it a more-meaningful—and therefore a more-energizing—experience for you?"

Farhan takes a few moments to think over the question. His answers to many of KC's questions come slowly, after due consideration. He's a reflective person. At last, he says, "I always thought that helping other people get better at their jobs would be very satisfying to me as a leader. I thought that would be meaningful for me."

"Then that's where we'll start. And we'll start small—one small step at a time."

"Baby steps. I can do baby steps," Farhan says with mounting confidence now that the tasks before him are starting to seem slightly more manageable.

"Of course you can. Now, I want you to pick just one member of your staff to focus your attentions on—someone who will appreciate your time and effort. That way, your chances for success are high. Who would that be?"

For the first time that day, Farhan's response is immediate. "Easy. I'd start with Heather. She's a sponge—just soaks up everything you tell her. And she really wants to improve. It's a clear desire in her."

"Heather it is!" KC says.

They reach the end of the park and circle back toward the bench where they first met, all the while discussing the particulars of Farhan's plan to help Heather develop her skills. They talk about various approaches and different ways to interact with her. As their discussion picks up steam, KC notices a lightness come over Farhan. His expression of disappointment vanishes, replaced by a look of excitement and engagement.

"I've heard about an approach called the GROW process," Farhan says. "That might be a good way to work with Heather. Are you familiar with it?"

"I absolutely am. Sir John Whitmore, a colleague of mine, developed the GROW model. I think it's a great technique to use here."

KC has often used the GROW model himself to incredible success. GROW functions as an acronym for goal, reality, options and will, which describes four distinct stages of development. The first stage is to clearly define a goal. The second stage is to acknowledge the reality of the situation, which includes identifying troublesome issues. The third stage is to come up with options for how to overcome these issues and problems. The final stage is to figure out what exactly you will do and when and how you will do it—to put the options into practice. It's a good system, and given Farhan's enthusiasm for it, KC is confident it can work.

Neither of them has so much as glanced at the time during this walk around the park, but when they arrive back at the bench, they pause and look at their wrist watches. It's much later than they'd thought. Both are happy with how things have gone. The change that has come over Farhan in the last ten minutes is proof enough of the value of their walk and their discussion. He's buoyant and excited. He agrees to get in touch with KC next week to let him know how things are going with Heather and how the plan is working.

Before they part ways, KC has one final question for him: "On a scale of one to ten, how energized do you feel by this plan?"

"I'm at an eleven," Farhan says, springing a little on his feet.

CHAPTER 10

CRISIS AT OPTIMAL IT

In this chapter, KC and Karen help develop Dominic's energy audit. Kenneth also teaches him about the transformative energy beneath the stories we tell ourselves, and Karen reluctantly learns of the power of an apology.

It's a beautiful sunny morning, and KC is about to head over to the fitness club. In his garage, he pulls the cover off his old restored MGB. This is the kind of morning to cruise with the top down in Mighty Mouse (as he's affectionately named his car). He doesn't get to use the old gal nearly as often as he'd like; the weather doesn't allow for it. She's a summer car, a fair-weather car, and for most of the year, all she does is take up space in his crowded garage.

"It's unbelievable to me that you, Mr. Practical, keep that car," Wanda says to him as he dusts off the car for its first drive in months. She's lodged this complaint a hundred times before. "It costs a fortune just to maintain it. And it's good to drive about five days a year."

"I can drive this baby five months of the year," he replies testily.

"I agree. Like I said, five times a year. Once a month for five months," she says with a healthy dose of sarcasm.

"You're exaggerating. It's perfectly practical."

Wanda softens her tone. "Look, Kenneth. You can justify keeping that car in a dozen ways, but practicality is not one of them. Even when the weather is perfect for the car, the situation isn't. Sometimes the trunk space isn't enough. Sometimes you're travelling too far to make the trip in this old thing. And sometimes—a lot of times, actually—you just don't want to bother uncovering it and getting it ready to go. It's inconvenient."

KC tries to devise a good counter to this reasonable assessment of things, when his cellphone rings and mercifully interrupts the conversation.

"Hello?" he says, answering the phone without even looking at the caller ID. He quickly retreats from the garage and from Wanda's annoyingly precise observations.

"Good morning, Kenneth," says Karen's cheery voice. "I'm guessing that I've caught you on your way to an early morning workout. Am I right?"

"And a good morning to you too, Karen. Your clairvoyance is bang on. I'm just on my way to the gym. But I get the feeling you aren't calling just to wish me a good workout. What's up?"

"Well, I'm afraid we've got a bit of an issue," she says. Her chipper tone from a moment before seems to have disappeared.

"Now it's my turn to be the clairvoyant," KC says. "I'm going to guess this issue has something to do with Dominic and Henri."

"Well, yes, of course. You nailed it."

"I should have an alternate career as a fortune-teller," he says, pleased with his guess.

"Let's not get carried away, Kenneth. It's not like you'd need particularly sharp intuitive skills to guess it has something to do with Henri. But let me fill you in on the details."

The major detail is that Henri has threatened to quit. He's isolated himself from the rest of the team. In spite of Henri's disruptive behaviour, the other programmers have all been making great progress, but even so, they haven't managed to catch up on the Metronome project. All of the stress has sent Dominic somewhere beyond the realm of frustration. He too has started making noise about maybe leaving Optimal IT.

"To be honest, Karen, I'm not surprised by this. And I'm sure you aren't either. I think we both knew the Henri situation was something we'd have to address sooner or later. He just has such a difficult personality."

"I know, I know. And you're right. I'm not surprised. I guess I've been dreading it."

"I'm sure you've already thought the situation through. So tell me. What do you think needs to happen next?"

"I'm big into the idea of eliminating the stressors and modifying the environment. But whenever I talk to Dominic about letting Henri go, he tells me that can't happen."

"Because?"

"Because he thinks Henri has a skill set that's absolutely necessary for the project. He thinks no one else has it. When I suggested reorganizing Henri's role so that he'd be less disruptive, Dominic nixed that idea too. He can't imagine how he might use Henri differently—not when he thinks about how Henri's skills need to be integrated into the overall project. The second part of all this—"

"There's a second part?"

"Yes. And that part is that Dominic is feeling like a failure as a manager."

"Because he can't handle Henri?"

"That's a big part of it for sure. You've got to remember that Dominic has been a successful manager for years. He really believes he should be able to handle this, to figure out a solution and make things better for everybody. You know, back when I was playing varsity volleyball, my sports psychologist had a term for what he's doing. She used to call it *shoulding* on yourself."

"Dominic's shoulding on himself?" KC asks, not sure he's heard her correctly.

"Yeah, you know, like 'I should be more patient. I shouldn't let Henri get to me. I should be able to figure something out. I should, I should …'"

"Ah, right. Shoulding."

"But all that does is create a sense of guilt. It chips away at his self-esteem. Quite frankly, I've never seen him so down. He actually told me he thinks he might be the issue. That's why he's thinking of quitting."

"I can tell you right now that Dominic's not the problem. I'm not sure I know anybody who would be immune to Henri's attitude and antics. We both know we really can't change Henri in any profound way, so what we've got to do is help Dominic become more resilient and less reactive. And that is definitely an energy management issue."

As their conversation continues, it sparks the memory of a wonderful series of books KC enjoyed reading when he was younger. The books, by Carlos Castaneda, detailed the author's tutelage under the Mexican Indian sorcerer Don Juan Matus. At one point in the books, Carlos is forced to deal with a petty tyrant, which, of course, proves to be a frustrating struggle. But the ever-wise Don Juan Matus sagely explains that a petty tyrant can often be more instructive than a master—that is, if the student can learn not to let the tyrant have an impact on him. He recounts this story from the books for Karen, who, unsurprisingly, is familiar with the series.

"There's a reason a lot of people call Castaneda's books fiction," Karen says. "What you're describing there is a pretty tall order. It might take several lifetimes for Dom to learn how not to let someone like Henri have any impact on him. And we need to help Dom now. So let's get practical here. What do you think we should do?"

From the tension brimming in Karen's tone, it's clear to KC that the situation at Optimal IT is strained. He's silent for a few moments while he tries to decide what technique would give them the best shot at achieving a breakthrough with Dominic. "We could begin by doing an energy audit on Dominic," he says at last.

"An energy audit? Is that a joke? Because I'm not laughing, Ken."

"I'm a hundred percent serious. I really think it could help."

"Well, all right. I have no idea what an energy audit is, but if you think it'll help, I'm on board. Should we meet to hammer out the details?"

"Sure. When do you want to do this?"

"Right now! I mean, if you can."

"Well, at the moment, I'm sort of—"

"Oh, that's right. You're just on your way to a workout. Sorry, Kenneth. Sorry. Get your workout in if you want. It's just that this is at the top of the heap for me right now, and I really need some help."

"Tell you what, Karen. I'll meet you in the lobby of the Crestwood Inn in fifteen minutes."

The Crestwood is a cute little hotel and restaurant on the way to KC's gym. He and his wife sometimes stop in there for brunch on the weekends. The place is nothing fancy but is pleasant, and it's not much of an inconvenience to make a quick pit stop at this familiar spot before he tackles the gym.

"Terrific, Ken. Thanks so much."

"But fair warning—you will be meeting with a man in gym shorts."

"I'll try to restrain myself," she says. "See you in fifteen."

There's a small restaurant off the lobby at the Crestwood Inn. KC hasn't had breakfast, so he sits down at a table and orders some muesli. He spoons the delicious dish and is about halfway through it when he sees Karen walk in and look around for him. He waves to get her attention, standing to make himself more noticeable, and when she at last spots him, her gaze immediately falls to his thin, bare legs.

"I see why you warned me about the shorts," she says as she takes a seat across from him. "Those might be the skinniest legs I've seen. Why don't you distract me by telling me about this energy audit?"

KC smiles. "I'll ignore your comments about my legs and get right into the audit. Now, this may sound a bit weird, but stay with me on this."

"Okay. But if it's really that weird, I'm going to need some coffee first," she says, flagging down a waiter, from whom she quickly orders a latte.

They chitchat briefly, and when the coffee arrives a few minutes later, she takes a big sip in preparation for the discussion. When she's sufficiently caffeinated, she looks him in the eyes and says, "All right. Let's have it. Energy audit."

"Okay. To start, let's think about Dominic as if he were a home—a house."

"Um, okay. He's a house," she says dubiously.

"Now we can analyze how energy-efficient he is. As the situation stands, when the temperature around him rises, he gets very hot. In other words, his energy level shoots way up—too far up. He's responding to the energy around him. He's very reactive. That's not the most-efficient setup. We can also observe some obvious energy leaks in Dominic, just as we could observe in a house. Dominic's not well insulated. His insulation is old and out of date. This is especially apparent when a big storm like Henri blows in. There's much better insulation available today. He needs an inner-skill update."

"Inner-skill update. Explain."

"When you were a varsity athlete, your sports psychologist helped strengthen your mental fitness skills, right?"

"Of course."

"Maybe she helped you become more resilient by giving you new ways of looking at what you were going through—new ways of interpreting pressure, for example."

"She did. That's true," Karen says.

"Well, that's an example of an inner-skill upgrade. But let's get back to our metaphor. The house is leaking energy because it's old and out of date. New thermostats and furnaces are much more energy efficient than the old ones—and much better at adapting to conditions. Just think of the old fan systems on heaters. They were either on or off. But new heating systems can heat a house very quickly, and once ideal temperatures are reached, they're able to maintain that temperature with subtle adjustments in both fan speed and energy expended. There's a variability and a flexibility at work there. Those are the very things Dominic needs."

Karen nods as she takes another sip of her latte. "I can't argue with that. I think we—"

Before she can finish that sentence, KC breaks in again. He's too excited about his metaphor to sit quietly and listen. He carries on with it, picking up more steam as he goes. "You see—Dominic needs to behave like a thermostat. He needs to learn to raise his temperature when the environment around him lacks energy, when it's cool. But he also needs to learn how to lower the temperature, or reduce his arousal level, when the environment is overly heated, when it's too intense. Mostly, Dominic needs to learn how to minimize the drain on his valuable resources. He needs a better-insulated house. And that house—"

"Enough, enough!" interrupts Karen. "I get the point. Let's not beat this metaphor to death."

"But I was just getting on a roll," KC says with a laugh, aware he might have gotten a bit carried away.

From behind her large latte cup, Karen fixes a highly unamused eye on him.

"Okay, okay," he admits. "So maybe I got swept up in the house thing. But the points are still valid. We need to meet with Dominic. We need a few sessions with him to work on the issues I just raised. Will he be open to that?"

"He's pretty open to anything at the moment. In my experience, when someone is drowning, they'll grasp at almost anything." Karen's expression changes slightly—a mischievous glint enters her eye. "Even a batt of insulation."

KC smiles. He deserves that bit of ribbing.

Later that afternoon, KC regroups with Karen, this time in Dominic's office—and this time in full-length pants instead of gym shorts.

Karen opens the meeting with kind words meant to ease Dominic's obvious agitation. "We're concerned about you, Dominic. That's why we're here."

Dominic nods, but he doesn't seem wholly comforted by this declaration. He's twitchy, even while sitting at his desk. His nervous energy has returned, and he can't seem to stop his eyes from darting around the desk or his fingers from picking up things to fiddle with—a pen, a paperclip, the little knickknacks scattered on his desk.

While Karen and Dominic exchange a few preliminary words, KC takes a second to look around the office. Piles of papers crowd his desk. Stacks of file folders edge the walls. If he had to describe the room in a word, it would be *cluttered*. KC spots a few framed photographs of Dominic's family—his wife and two kids—on the radiator shelf. In one of the photographs, the whole family is squashed into the frame, all giving easy smiles and looking happy. The backdrop of the shot is a gorgeous cornfield. KC figures the photo must have been taken sometime in late summer, judging by the sunlight and the height of the corn stalks. It's a lovely picture.

"I want to hear from you, Dominic," KC says. "Tell me what's going on with the department right now."

"Henri is what's going on. I don't know what else to say."

"Well, let's explore that. What exactly is it like to manage him?"

Dominic gazes out the window for a moment while he thinks about how best to describe the situation. "You know, it's sort of like this. It's like I'm trying to plow a field, and there's a huge boulder in the middle of that field. I can't get a good flow going, because that big boulder keeps getting in the way. And I'm constantly aware of where the boulder is. I'm always trying to find ways around it."

KC is struck by how apt this metaphor is. From an earlier conversation, he remembers that Dominic grew up on a farm. Dominic understands the business of ploughing fields and the obstacles that present themselves in that endeavour. It's no wonder this analogy is how he's decided to describe his current situation

"How does that feel? When you're trying to plough that field, but the boulder keeps interfering with your progress?"

"Well, it's obviously incredibly frustrating. It takes away any sense of accomplishment I might have. I keep wishing and wanting it to be another way—better, easier. I don't know."

Since Dominic is at home in the language of fields and boulders, KC decides to roll with the metaphor. "You can see the impact this boulder is having on you, right? There's nothing to be gained by allowing it to frustrate you or sap you of your energy."

"No, I guess there's not."

Dominic can see the effect Henri is having on him and on his team, but he still needs to learn how to separate himself from what he's going through in any given moment. He needs some psychological hygiene.

To this end, KC decides to perform the same exercise with Dominic that he did with the basketball players at the training camp in Edmonton. He asks him to describe what happens at the body, feelings and mind levels when things aren't working well.

Dominic is quick to grasp the distinction between these three levels. "I'll start with the feelings level," he says. "Just because my feelings are so strong at the moment."

"Great. Let's hear what happens when you're having a particularly tough time with Henri."

"I feel frustrated and upset. And angry."

"What about at the mind level?" KC asks.

"Well, when I think of the mind, I guess I think about my self-talk. When things aren't going well with Henri, that self-talk usually revolves around how I should be able to handle this, how I should be doing a better job and how unfair it all is. Well, as you can tell, everything's a bit of a jumble."

"Not at all. I'm following what you're saying. What about the body level?"

Dominic takes a moment to let out a big sigh before he tackles this one. "At the body level, well, I guess that's where the trouble is most obvious. In the really intense moments, I cross my arms tightly, and I feel my face get all red. Sometimes I feel like I'm on fire because I'm so hot. I feel very strong, too. I don't know how to describe that exactly. It's like something is gripping inside my chest."

KC is again impressed with Dominic's descriptive abilities. "That's a very vivid picture, Dom. It must be extremely hard on you."

"It's hard on me, yeah. But it's even harder on those around me.

I'm just not a competent leader when I'm in that state. And even worse, when I get home, I'm not happy. My family picks up on that. Who wouldn't, really?"

Dominic drops his head and stares intently at the paperclip he's been toying with for the last few minutes. Replaying the effects of these draining encounters with Henri seems to have exhausted him.

KC waits a moment to let the tension in the room settle and then says, "Dominic, I hear what you're going through. Can I give you some information that might be helpful in terms of your perspective—that is, how you're looking at the situation?"

Dominic nods, but even that simple movement seems to cost him a great deal of energy.

"You're clearly a very caring person. That's obvious from what you've just said and from everything else I know about you. But it's important that you make a distinction between yourself, who you are and all of the stuff that's happening to you. The things you've just told me don't define who you are. They just describe the situation you're facing."

"I'm not sure I follow. I mean, that red-faced guy I described—that's me!"

"It's part of you, yes. But it's not a full picture."

To better illustrate his point, KC tells a story of a figure skater he worked with at a World Championships years ago. About fifteen minutes before she was set to take the ice, the skater told KC she was nervous.

"Okay. But what else are you?"

At first, she looked dumbfounded. "What?"

"Well, for example, how's your confidence been?"

"Great. It's been great."

"And your fitness level?"

"Yeah, it's great too."

"And how has your training gone this week?"

"It's gone really well, actually."

KC asked her a few more questions, and each time, he elicited a positive response. Finally, he said to her, "So your confidence is great, you're very fit, your training is awesome and you love the program you're about to skate—and you're a little nervous. It's important to remember all of who we are, not just what we're experiencing in the moment. We forget that. We focus only on our feelings or thoughts. And if we're not careful, we can become what we're experiencing. So we have to learn to separate ourselves from our experiences."

While KC recounts this story, he notices Karen sitting quietly but attentively. As he finishes, she takes her opportunity to speak up.

"Dominic," she says, "I've known you a long time. Aside from the fact that you're a good human being, you've got a million qualities that make you an exceptional manager. In that first group session we did with KC, so many of your team members commented on how well you dealt with Henri when you were in his group. They felt protected by you. And I can guarantee you no one at this company wants to lose you."

Dominic raises his eyes to look at her. He's clearly moved by her words. "Okay. So how do we fix this?" he asks.

Over the next week, KC and Dominic meet several times for one-on-one sessions. KC works with him just as he would work with an elite athlete. They begin by working on perspective skills. It's important for Dominic to understand that he projects his experiences from one situation onto other unrelated situations. To combat this tendency, KC suggests he take a few minutes after every interaction with Henri to debrief himself, get a better perspective on what just happened and centre himself. In this way, his exchanges with Henri won't bleed into his interactions with others.

In their second session together, they develop what Dominic later calls the Feelings Plan, which arises from Dominic's difficulty in understanding how to control his feelings.

"I don't always want to feel what I'm feeling. But what else can I do? I can't exactly control that sort of thing. Feelings just happen," Dominic says.

"Feelings don't just come out of the sky, Dominic. They come from the stories we tell ourselves—or, to be more specific, the parts of the stories that we begin to imagine. Because the minute we begin to imagine, we generate feelings and emotions. And beneath every emotion, there's energy—the energy to move forward, to transform."

On a piece of paper, KC draws a tidy flowchart detailing this process. The chart reads as follows:

Stories
Imagination
Feelings/Emotions
Energy

With his chin resting on his fist, Dominic studies the flowchart for a minute. "So what this is saying is that if I adjust the stories I tell myself, I can adjust my energy levels?" Dominic asks.

"Bang on. That's exactly it. But let's take a look at how this works, step by step."

"I'm all for that."

"The first thing we need to do, as you pointed out, is change the stories we tell ourselves, or at least ask ourselves whether these stories are true. For example, let's say Karen says to me, 'KC, you need to start pulling your weight.' Well, when I imagine that, I start to get upset, because I've already started telling myself a story. Maybe I tell myself that she doesn't realize all the hard work I do. She doesn't know what I'm up against. She doesn't like me. Maybe she never has. It goes on and on. Now, when I run into you later in the day, I might say to you, 'Karen said some stuff to me that really ticked me off!' But to be picky, that isn't exactly true. The truth of the matter is that I angered myself as a result of what I imagined— the stories I told myself after my interaction with Karen. Most of what caused my hurt and angry feelings was fabricated by me, by my mind."

"Now, hold on a minute there, KC. You're saying, in this hypothetical situation, Karen didn't make you angry? That you made yourself angry? Is that true? I mean, it's Karen's fault, isn't it?"

"Karen is at fault, as a leader, only in that she was reactive and didn't communicate in a respectful or appropriate manner. But I was the one who made myself angry."

"And you did that by?"

"By creating particular stories. Let me use another example. Let's say you and I have been told that we have to do a presentation to senior management. We meet to talk immediately after this announcement has been made to us. You're excited and feeling challenged by the possibility, whereas I'm just nervous and anxious. We both heard the same message, but we have very different feelings about it."

"Because I'm telling myself very different stories about what's about to happen than you're telling yourself. Is that right?"

"Precisely," says KC. Seeing how quickly Dominic is grasping the concept, he decides to take the idea a step further.

"Now, let's go back to the first example. Suppose you were to ask me what I thought triggered Karen into saying what she did. In trying to answer that question, I might start to imagine that she met with her boss, Douglas, who was frustrated with how long the whole process was taking. Maybe he yelled at her. So she comes out of that meeting feeling put down and angry, and she runs into me in the hall, and there I am, joking around with Kate. When I start to imagine that scenario, it creates a whole different set of feelings and emotions in me, because it's a very different story.

"Maybe I start to imagine what might have happened to Karen in her childhood that led to her having a short fuse. That story also leads to a different emotional state in me. The point is, the stories we tell ourselves lead to the emotions we feel, and often, those stories aren't the truth—at least not the whole truth. Many of the things that cause us to doubt or worry or stress are imaginary. When we change the story, we change the feelings."

"And when we change the feelings, we change the energy," Dominic says, finishing for him.

"You got it."

Dominic smiles and looks back down at the flowchart, as if to make sure it's firmly inscribed in his memory.

When KC arrives for their third session later that week, he finds the flowchart taped up on a wall of Dominic's office, right above the photographs of his family.

"You've done some redecorating," KC says.

Dominic offers up a shy smile. "I'm eager to see what gems you have for me today."

"Well, today I thought I'd start with a story about a woman I heard speak in San Diego a while back. Her name's Olivia Fox Cabane."

Olivia's talk addressed the issue of self-confidence, and how self-critical many people are, particularly those who are highly educated. For KC, one of the highlights of the talk was when she referenced a study in which the researches asked an MBA class at Stanford how many of them believed themselves to be, in effect, impostors. About 80 percent of the attendees raised their hands.

"That's a lot of people doubting themselves," Dominic says.

"It sure is. And the real problem with self-criticism is that it affects your body language."

"How's that?"

KC explains how it's impossible to fully control your body language. Body language is simply a reflection of what you're imagining and saying to yourself. Self-criticism can cause a physical reaction—maybe in your eyes or your expression—and others often misinterpret this reaction. You might be scowling because of what's happening internally, but others see that scowl as a reaction to them.

In her talk, Olivia also pointed out that difficult people are often self-critical. Because of this, you need to find something you like about them before you engage with them. That way, their expressions—their scowls, glowers or frowns—won't trigger defensive body language in you. If you imagine something positive about them, the thought keeps your body language positive and helps you deal with them.

As KC discusses this concept, Dominic's expression brightens until his excitement for the idea is too much to contain. He interrupts KC midsentence in a burst of hopeful enthusiasm. "Henri is highly educated and very difficult, so maybe he's one of those people who's super self-critical. I just need to find something I like about him and remember that before my next meeting with him."

As Dominic searches, wide-eyed and smiling, for a scrap of paper on which to make a note of this idea, KC feels worried.

"Uh-oh," KC mutters to himself. "I may have overshot things here. Maybe next time I should introduce the skill of letting go."

Dominic doesn't hear these quiet utterances. He's busy imagining his next meeting with Henri, buoyed by this hope of improvement.

"About Henri," KC ventures. "I know you want to hold on to him. But we also need to consider alternatives."

"There is no alternative. I need his skill set."

"There are always alternatives. For instance, could a consultant replace Henri's encryption knowledge? Someone more congenial? Someone who could work with and educate the team?"

Dominic isn't ready to accept this suggestion as a solution. "I don't know. Henri's very skilled."

"Mm-hmm," KC says.

"And really, I think I'm getting better at dealing with him since you and I started these sessions. I'd like to stick with him."

"Sticking with the giant boulder," KC says quietly to himself.

Late Friday afternoon, after his last session of the week with Dominic, KC drops by Karen's office for an impromptu visit. Standing in the doorway, KC can see she's not her usual self today. She's bad tempered and irritable, and when he presses her about it, she reveals that an argument with her sister, Kathy, has set her off kilter.

"Want to talk about it?" he asks, maintaining his position at the door in case she prefers to be alone.

"Well, I don't know. Maybe. I guess so," she says, fidgeting in her chair. She's in the mood to slouch, but she's also too worked up and irritated to commit to that posture. Finally, she settles into what looks like an uncomfortable position and gears up to vent. "My sister and I have different views on almost everything. Everything!

This time, it's about my mother. She's in a nursing home. I won't give you all the gory details, but Kathy and I really got into it this time. Usually when she's being her bossy self, I manage to stay calm and deal with her, but this time, it involves our mother and her health, and on this issue, I'm just not willing to compromise with my sister. I pretty much lost it. Said some things I wish I hadn't. But they're no worse than the things she says to me all the time. I guess I got down to her level. And I'm not proud of it."

"So not only are you upset with your sister, but you're also not very happy with your own behaviour."

"Yes, that's what I just said," she says, her voice clipped and harsh. "I don't need a recap. I need advice."

KC doesn't bat an eye. He knows exactly what she needs to do. "You'll have to apologize to your sister."

"Apologize to her! What! I'm telling you that she's incredibly difficult to deal with, and your advice for me is to apologize? Haven't you heard a thing I've said?" Karen exclaims.

"I've heard what you've said—every word. And my entire focus is on you—believe me," KC says. He gently closes the door to her office and takes a seat at her desk, directly across from her. "You're not happy with the way you behaved. You have no control over your sister, but you can do something about your own behaviour. You can do something to improve your feelings about that aspect of things."

"Kenneth, not everything in this world is an energy management issue," she says with a trace of venom. "I'm just going to let this go and move on—the way I always do with her."

"Karen, I couldn't care less about your sister. But I do care about you, and you're not yourself at the moment. This isn't something you're just going to let go of. Letting go is a terrific energy management skill when there's nothing you can do about the situation or the person involved. But in this instance, there is something you can do. Because you're angry with yourself."

"I'm also angry with my sister. Keep up, Kenneth."

"One thing at a time, Karen. An apology will free you of your anger with yourself. And the way I see it, there's an opportunity here."

"An opportunity? How so?"

"If I understand things correctly, Kathy always behaves sort of terribly. You say that you lowered yourself to her level. That's not where you want to stay. With an apology, you might even be able to influence her in moving more toward your level."

"I hate being the one who always takes the high road," she says, exasperated at the thought of having to rise to that position yet again. "She's so controlling that she'll probably see my apology as a victory. And I have no intention of showing her any weakness by apologizing."

KC allows himself a slight shake of the head. How often people view apologies as signs of weakness. But they're usually the opposite. "In this case, Karen, an apology is a tremendous show of strength. Not only will it allow you to let go of your regret about your own behaviour, but it's a clear demonstration of your desire to move to higher ground in terms of how you two communicate."

Karen blows out a frustrated breath, but she sits up a little taller in her chair. "I'm starting to see your point—reluctantly."

They take a few minutes to discuss how to orchestrate an effective apology to her sister. KC points out the three steps to a good apology. Number one is admitting you were wrong and are sorry. Number two is making it clear you understand the impact your behaviour has had. Number three is making it clear you're going to do things differently in the future, that this won't happen again.

He adds, "An effective apology requires that you prepare what you're going to say, so you can deliver it the way you intend to. It's easy to get blown off course."

"I can see that. Especially when I imagine Kathy reacting in her usual way. I need a plan that lays out not only what I'm going to say but also how I'm going to manage myself."

"Exactly. You want some help with that?"

"Let me draft what I'm going to say. If I need your help, I'll e-mail it to you for your comments. Is that all right?"

KC nods as he makes his way back to the door of the office. When he gets to the door, he pauses and looks back at her. "Here's some extra advice. Try your best to leave out words like *pond scum* and *varmint* if you can," he teases.

"Jeez, it sounds like you know my sister!" she says, a smile finally beginning to emerge.

KC never gets a draft of the apology, but the e-mail he does get from Karen later that night is even better. It's a short note that reads,

> You were right. It was an energy management
> issue. I feel like a piano is off my back. Thanks!

He reads the message twice and then turns off his computer with a smile. It's been a long day—a long week. It's time to catch up on some rest.

CHAPTER 11

SECOND SHOW

In this chapter, KC wakes up the radio audience—and Bill—with scintillating information on the importance of sleep, naps and other exciting things.

The rain drums on the roof of the car as KC makes his way to the radio station for the second show. KC has always loved this sound. Listening to the steady pitter-patter of the rain reminds him of the naps he used to take at his cottage on rainy afternoons.

Decades ago, KC and Wanda hosted a figure skater he'd been working with—Caitlyn—at their cottage. Caitlyn arrived with her husband and 3-month-old baby girl, Julia, in tow. It was a fun weekend filled with good company, good food, games and conversation. But what KC remembers most fondly about that weekend is relaxing on his recliner with little baby Julia sound asleep on his chest. With the rain playing a gentle tune on the metal roof of his cottage, it wasn't more than a few minutes before he joined the baby in a long, peaceful sleep.

As KC peers through the rain streaking his windshield, this nostalgic reflection transforms into a broader musing on the importance of good rest. It's not surprising that his thoughts would wander in this direction today. This is the topic of today's show, after all: rest and recovery. KC is eager to get the show under way—there's nothing as exciting as talking about sleep.

When he arrives in the studio, Bill is already there, leaning back in his chair, his feet up on the table, his eyes half closed. He looks tired but manages a lazy wave at KC.

"How are you on this rainy afternoon?" KC asks, taking his seat beside him.

Bill throws out a dismissive hand, keen to do away with friendly preliminaries. He has more-pressing concerns. "Let's skip all that, Ken. I want to know—how are things working out with Farhan?"

"Oh, good, good. We met up, and we put a plan together. I actually just got a text from him. He's got a management question he wants to ask me after the show today."

"Wait. What? A question about management? I thought the issue was his son and the soccer game. Wasn't that it? Did I dream that? Am I losing my mind?" he says, laughing slightly and scratching his head.

"Rest easy, Bill; you're not losing your mind. The son's soccer game was definitely real, and it was a clear symptom of underlying problems. But it's not the core issue."

"Oh. So what's the core issue?"

"Well, look, we can talk about all this later. Right now, I need to review my introductory notes for the show's opening," KC says as he pulls notes from his bag. He lays the pages out on the table and quickly goes over what he's written. "Did you get these notes, Bill? I e-mailed them to you last night."

"Yeah, I did," Bill says, tilting to the left to scan the pages on the table. He smiles slyly and adds, "But you know, I couldn't help but notice that you sent them awfully late. You weren't, by chance, burning the midnight oil preparing for your talk about rest and recovery, were you, Ken? Not exactly practicing what you preach. You know, that's something I might bring up on air today!"

"Do what you have to do, my friend," KC says, and then he leans a little closer to Bill, making a show of examining his tired expression, searching for traces of fatigue. "Are those dark circles under your eyes, Bill? Looks like you might have had a late night yourself. Better pay attention today. I may have some ammunition of my own."

This lighthearted fencing between Bill and KC spills over into the show. KC spends the first five minutes presenting the material mapped out in his notes. He outlines—perhaps in too much detail—how important sleep is and how deprived of adequate recovery many people are.

"So what you're saying is to never skimp on the sleep?" Bill asks.

"I just can't stress enough how important it is. You know, Harvard's very own sleep doctor, Charles Czeisler, says that skipping sleep is like working while drunk," KC says.

"Without the great buzz no doubt," adds Bill.

"No doubt. But there's a lot of science behind all this. When we sleep, we go through ninety- to one-hundred-twenty-minute cycles. And within those cycles, there are two main types of sleep: deep sleep and rapid eye movement, or REM, sleep."

KC takes his time describing the distinction. Deep sleep dominates the early stages of a cycle as the brain consolidates memories and builds up stores of energy. As time goes on, however, REM sleep becomes predominant. This is when we dream. Many studies have pointed out that adequate deep sleep is crucial for integrating new memories. In an ideal world, we'd sleep immediately after learning something, because the sleep would help consolidate that information. Obviously, this isn't always possible. But it's important to note that when we're sleep deprived, we miss a lot of opportunities to integrate these new memories. Therefore, sleep isn't just about rest and recovery; it's also about skill development. It's about getting better at performance—particularly when that performance involves memory.

Without realizing it, KC has been talking for minutes without pause. When he finally does stop, he looks over at Bill, who's slouched in his chair again and yawning.

"I guess I've been going on a bit long here," KC says with a laugh. "Too long-winded?"

Bill, caught slightly off guard by this sudden address, bounces forward in his chair and says, "Oh no. Of course not, Ken. But I'm worried all this sleep talk is going to have exactly the desired effect. It's going to put our listeners right to sleep."

"Are you suggesting I'm boring?"

"Oh, I'd never suggest that! Let's just say your lecture here has been incredibly persuasive—so persuasive and so very detailed that you'll have our listeners switching off the radio and taking afternoon naps. So let's take a quick commercial break, and when we come back, we'll liven things up with a few callers."

"No argument here. It might be nice to hear someone else's voice for a change," KC says with good cheer.

When they come back from the break, they head straight to the switchboards. The first call they take comes from Nikki, a third-year commerce student at a local university.

"Hey there, Nikki. You've got a question for Kenneth?" Bill asks.

"Yeah, I do. The thing is, I have a problem with all-nighters," she says.

"Ah, the dreaded all-nighter. I know it well," KC says.

"Our profs always stress not to pull all-nighters before exams. But honestly, does it really make that much of a difference what time of the day—or night—we do our studying as long as we're putting in the time? Sometimes there really isn't much choice in the matter. I mean, I'm swamped with schoolwork and extracurriculars. It's a miracle I find the time to even get through all my studying."

It's clear from Nikki's tone that she's hoping KC will validate her late-night cramming sessions. But the facts don't allow him to offer her that satisfaction.

"Sorry to be the bearer of bad news, Nikki. But yes, the time of day you study absolutely makes a difference. And all-nighters are a bad idea on a couple of fronts. First off, you'll be sleep deprived on the day of your exam, so you'll be writing the exam in a drunken state. Second, when you cram material, you're a lot less likely to retain any of the information you learned."

"I was afraid you were going to say that," she says with a big sigh, disappointed by the reality of the situation. "But you know, Kenneth, exam season is so busy. And not just for me. I know it's the same for a lot of students. We're expected to attend regular lecture hours, polish off end-of-term essays and group presentations and keep up with all of our responsibilities on whatever volunteer committees we're on, and on top of it all, we're supposed to find time to master an entire course load of material! And somehow, magically, we're supposed to fit in a solid eight hours of sleep! Impossible."

Not a stranger to this dilemma, KC is able to empathize. He remembers the almost-never-ending stream of work that came his way while working toward his PhD. "Nikki, you mentioned group presentations in your list of to-dos. Do you think that might be an area where you could lighten your load? Team presentations allow group members to delegate responsibilities so that no one person is left doing the entire project alone. If you organize it right, could you maybe find a way to make those projects less time-consuming?"

"You'd think that," Nikki says. "But the team-based project structure can add stress just as easily as it can relieve it. In the best of circumstances, when you're assigned to a driven and highly motivated group, you still end up sinking a lot of time into coordinating meeting times with all the members. I mean, we're all overinvolved. We all have a million commitments—sports teams, part-time jobs, whatever. So it's a nightmare to organize our schedules. That's why we often resort to holding meetings at weird hours of the night. I once didn't leave campus until six o'clock in the morning because of a late-night team meeting. That's how it is in my program anyway. All-nighters have really become part of the commerce culture. And when everyone around you is putting in late night hours, it's hard not to feel guilty if you're not doing that too."

From the increasingly strained notes in her voice, KC can tell she's nearing the end of her rope. The hectic schedule is starting to fray her nerves, and it's annihilating her energy. Her issue presents a lot of interesting angles from an energy management perspective, and KC finds himself wishing he had a few minutes, maybe a commercial break, to think things over. Then, as if reading his mind, Bill interjects.

"This is one doozy of an issue, Nikki. I'm sure Dr. C here will have some sound advice for you. But before we unleash him on you, we need to hear a few words from our sponsors—they're keeping us on the air, after all! Hang in there, Nikki. We'll be right back with you."

During the break, KC quietly reflects on Nikki's issues. Bill generously helps promote an atmosphere of quiet contemplation by leaning back in his chair and closing his eyes. The poor guy must have had a late night. As KC thinks over the many variables of Nikki's situation, he decides he has a few questions he'd like to put to her before he offers any advice. He needs more details about her situation.

Just as the commercials come to end, Bill opens his eyes and sits up straight, as if divining the exact moment he has to be back on air. "Hey there. We're back with Dr. Kenneth Coghill," he says. "Today we're talking about sleep, and we've got Nikki on the line. Nikki, you still with us?"

"Yeah, I'm right here."

"Nikki, let me ask you something," KC says, taking control of the conversation once more. "Does your university do anything to acknowledge the pressure you students are under? Does it provide any resources to help you deal with them?"

"Hmm, well, I don't know if this qualifies, but they do bring in petting animals to help reduce stress."

"Petting animals?" says Bill. "Help me out here, Nikki. That's not something I remember from my college days."

"Oh. Well, you know, like puppies, kittens, lambs. They bring the animals onto campus, and for about twenty minutes you get to sort of hang out with them. Pet them. Cuddle them. It really does reduce stress. But the effect doesn't last very long, unfortunately."

"Well, Doc? You got anything stronger than puppy love?" Bill asks, turning to look at KC.

"There's a lot to think about here. Nikki, you've raised some concerns that hit on aspects of energy management outside of what we're discussing here today—comparing yourself to other students, feeling guilty. We'll cover these issues next month, when we talk about minimizing the drain on energy resources. But for now, let me stick with the issue of sleep."

"Sounds good. The sleep thing is my biggest problem at the moment anyway."

"I don't doubt that. When you're not sleeping properly, it's hard for anything else to work properly. But with some proper organization, there are ways this issue could play in your favour."

KC reviews Nikki's situation for the show's listeners. Given her academic load and the fact that she's having team meetings during what should be sleep hours, it's obvious she's not on a regular sleep schedule. Adequate sleep every 24-hour cycle is critical. Nikki's daytime schedule is firmly set—there's not much she can do to change things there—and her late-night hours are also often slammed, so if she knows she's going to be up into those wee-morning hours, she'll have to find other times to sleep—even if that means grabbing a few hours around dinnertime. It's not ideal, but it's better than going a whole 24-hour cycle without any shut-eye at all.

On the upside, because research has made it clear that sleeping immediately after studying helps the brain solidify the knowledge, Nikki can amplify her studying efforts by sleeping directly after a study session whenever possible. She might also consider taking naps during the day, maybe between classes. Naps, coupled with a strong relaxation procedure, can help her stay rested and relaxed.

"But I want to be very clear here, Nikki. This has to be a temporary state of affairs. As soon as it's workable, you need to get back to a regular sleep schedule. That means a good, solid sleep every night."

"Okay. I think I can do that."

"And one last thing," he says. "Just a bit of studying advice."

"Sure. I'll take all the help I can get."

For this last piece of advice, KC draws from Sian Beilock's book *Choke*. Beilock suggests that in studying for exams or tests, it's best to study under the same conditions as those under which you'll be tested. So for example, if the exam will be timed and written without study aids, it's a good idea to impose those same conditions on some of your study sessions. This approach will help you get used to what you'll experience on exam day. Testing yourself on the material rather than simply studying it helps you remember it better in the long run.

"I hope that helps, Nikki."

"Oh, it does. I really think it does. Thanks, Kenneth."

After tying things up with Nikki, Bill introduces a second caller to the conversation: a young air-traffic controller named Fernando.

"Hi there, Fernando, and welcome," KC says.

"So what can the doc help you with today?" asks Bill.

Fernando begins by acknowledging how important it is that he be well rested in order to perform his job well. "There's a lot at stake. If I fall asleep or even just doze off for a minute, it can be a huge problem—a life-threatening problem for people on those planes. And yet, still, I'm just not managing to get enough sleep."

"Can you tell me why not?" KC asks.

"I wish I knew why not. I do try to get to bed on time. But I have so much trouble actually falling asleep. My days are just so busy; there's a lot going on, and I've always got so many things on my mind by the time I get to bed. I have a heck of a time getting to sleep sometimes. Hours and hours pass, and nothing. I'm still wide awake, just staring at the ceiling. Any advice about that? Apart from counting sheep, that is. Because at this point, I must have counted a few million sheep."

"I totally understand this caller's problem, Doc," Bill says. "I've done my share of sheep counting, and it's always a bust. What about it, Ken? Can you give us the cure to insomnia?"

"I have to say, Bill, it's hard to believe you could have insomnia problems. Even now, you already seem half-asleep," KC teases.

"Nonsense. This is just what I look like when I'm focusing."

"Well, at the risk of straining your *focus*, I'm going to answer Fernando's question in some detail. You may not need to follow every single one of these tips, Fernando, but research tells us these things are incredibly helpful for getting people to fall asleep."

"I'm all ears."

KC begins a lengthy explanation of how to create an environment most conducive for achieving a peaceful, uninterrupted night's sleep. One factor to consider is room temperature. A good temperature for sleep is somewhere between 60 and 67 degrees. This atmosphere will help the body relax.

A second important factor is light. A perfectly dark room is ideal. That means no sunlight but also no light from electronic devices—cellphones, alarm clocks, TVs. These gadgets emit bits of light that interrupt sleep. A phone on the nightstand can easily cause you to wake up frequently during the night if the phone lights up with notifications—whether you're consciously aware of them or not. It's a good idea to pare down the stimulating effect of electronics a full hour before your desired bedtime. Stimulating the brain right before bed can make sleep more elusive and challenging.

Then, of course, there's noise. Obviously, it's best to reduce noise as much as possible. Turn off the TV. Close the windows. Shut out sounds from the outside world.

Once KC has detailed this list of environmental factors, he moves on to the importance of creating a presleep routine. Regardless of how hard we try, it's impossible to force ourselves to fall asleep, but we can force ourselves to become more relaxed, which will increase our chances of falling asleep. Relaxation techniques, such as progressive muscle relaxation and deep breathing, can help us drift off more effectively and efficiently.

When KC pauses here, Bill takes his chance to break in. "So, Fernando, anything from this list—this long list—strike you as usable?"

Fernando laughs and says, "Well, yeah, pretty much everything. I guess I don't do any of the things I should. And I do almost all of the things I shouldn't. But I do have a question."

"Fire away," KC says.

"I'm not sure what you mean by progressive muscle relaxation. Can you tell me what that is exactly?"

"Oh, for sure. Let me explain. This is a technique created many years ago by a guy named Jacobson. It's actually very simple to understand. You start with your left foot—your toes. Tighten your toes, flex them and contract the muscles down there. Hold that contraction for two or three seconds. Then release the muscle and allow your feet and toes to relax fully. Next, do the same with your right foot. Then do your left calf muscle and then your right calf muscle. Basically, you move your way up your body until you get to your forehead."

"Seems simple enough."

"It is. It's very simple. That's one of the best things about it. And it's helpful in a lot of ways. For one, it pulls your attention away from whatever it is you're thinking about it—whatever's distracting you from sleep. It also allows you to release tension in various parts of your body, getting the whole body ready for sleep. Once you've done this a few times, you'll probably be able to relax your leg simply by visualizing that practiced relaxation. That's called autogenic training. It really sets you up well for falling asleep—provided, of course, you've created the right environmental conditions."

KC sneaks a look at Bill and is happy, if slightly surprised, to see him starting to look more alert. Bill asks, "Does this work for naps too, Ken? Could one use these techniques to get ready for a nap?"

"Of course. The same principles apply."

At this point, Fernando springs back into the conversation. He asks, "Since you've brought up naps, mind if I ask a few questions about this subject?"

"Happy to hear your questions," KC says. "I love discussing naps. Almost as much as I like taking them."

"I like them too," Fernando says. "But is there any science about how long a nap should be? Because I feel like if I nap for too long—say, an hour—I wake up all groggy. And then I'm even more tired than I was before I took the nap."

"You know, maybe I should let Bill answer this," KC says with a sidelong smile at Bill. "He seems to be the master of the five-minute nap. Every commercial break, he closes his eyes and seems to drift off."

"I'm not napping. Just studying the backs of my eyelids," Bill says, defending himself.

"Call it what you will, Bill. It's a terrific thing to do. I've always considered myself a sort of nap expert. My youngest son once even gave me a T-shirt that read, 'I love to party, and by *party*, I mean *nap*.' But I think you might have me beat in the napping department, Bill."

"I don't know about that. I've never been given a T-shirt," Bill jokes.

KC laughs lightly before diving back into things with Fernando. He explains that the part of the nap cycle—or the sleep cycle—you wake up in determines whether or not you wake up feeling groggy. If you wake up in the middle of a sleep cycle, no matter how much sleep you've achieved up till then, you'll get out of bed feeling ill rested. But if you wake up near the end of the cycle, you'll feel wide awake and ready to take on the day.

"There's actually a great technological innovation called the Sleep Cycle alarm clock, an app that analyzes your movement and sleep quality throughout the night," KC says.

"The future is upon us," says Bill.

"Isn't it exciting? And it's been a great investment—let me tell you. Ninety-nine cents for the world's best alarm clock. I program it with a rough idea of when I want to wake up, and it wakes me up at the end of the sleep cycle closest to that time. I always wake up feeling great! Now, in terms of naps, if you want to avoid grogginess altogether, it's best to try to limit nap time to under thirty minutes. Do you think you could take half-hour naps at work, Fernando?"

"I could maybe find the time for it, yeah. But I'm not sure where exactly I'd take these naps. It's not like there are beds at work," says Fernando.

Finding places to take midday naps isn't the easiest task. KC knows this from experience. He's been known to sneak a nap in his car or in an unoccupied lounge or office. Neither of those are ideal nap locations, but they're certainly not the worst either. He recently read an article about workers finding much-worse, though more-creative, places to nap. He decides to share this story with Fernando.

"I've got a funny story for you, Fernando," he says. "There was an interesting article in the *Wall Street Journal* a little while back about how junior interns working at a major American bank were dealing with this very problem. The article reported an increase of sleep-related problems for junior interns. But it also found an interesting increase in the number and length of washroom breaks among the interns. After a few interviews, it became clear that the interns were actually using their allotted washroom breaks to get rest. It's a phenomenon rather appropriately termed *toilet napping*. These interns would head to the washroom, plug their headphones into their phones, set alarms and lean their heads against the wall of the stall. And they'd nap right there!"

"Oh, I believe it. I can definitely see that happening," says Bill. "Even here at the station, we've started piping the radio into the washrooms so that the announcers, hosts and DJs from our various shows will get back to the studio after commercial breaks. It's a policy we instituted after a few of them overstayed their washroom time. I've always suspected they were doing what you call toilet napping."

"I'd like to go on the record as saying I'm not highly recommending toilet napping. There are other more appropriate—and more comfortable—options," says KC.

For the first time this afternoon, Bill seems lively. "You know, I remember a guy we had on the show a while back. He'd invented a sort of napping pod for offices. The pod looks a bit like a reclined first-class airline seat with a hood over the head section."

"I know exactly what you mean," KC says. "I think there are several designs for those kinds of pods. The one I tried was called MetroNaps EnergyPod. More and more companies are starting to put these devices in their offices. They're realizing the importance of their employees recharging. Certainly, if you ask any group in any workplace if they'd be more productive if they could crash for ten or fifteen minutes in the afternoon, the vast majority of them would say yes."

Nodding vigorously, Bill adds, "But this is all sort of *Back to the Future* stuff, isn't it? I mean, napping is an old practice in some parts of the world. A bunch of cultures have had siestas for centuries.

Once again, we might not be quite as modern as we think. Heck, the Aztecs and Mayans were centuries ahead of us."

"It's true. And it's a lot easier to get in the habit of napping when it's a culturally accepted practice. Many people I speak to still feel they have to do it privately, even secretly. So they go down to their cars in an underground garage, or if they can, they lock their office doors and lie back in their chairs for ten, maybe fifteen, minutes. These options, however, aren't available to everyone."

"But they should be. They really should be," says Fernando. "Especially in a job like mine, where sleep is so important. Why not make sure that we're all well rested?"

"Oh, I couldn't agree more," KC says. "And I happen to believe that these kinds of options soon will be offered to more and more workers. We just can't continue asking people to work harder and do more and then not provide them with an opportunity to rest. They need to be able to pull the saw blade out of the wood to sharpen the saw. You cut more wood with that sharper blade."

"Sage words, Doc," interrupts Bill. "And I think this is as good a place as any to take our last break. Fernando, I hope some of this discussion has helped."

"Definitely. Thanks, guys."

During the last break, KC glances at the clock and sees it's almost the top of the hour. This second show flew by even faster than the first. When they get back on air, they have time for just one more caller. It's a young woman again this time, another university student. Sleep—or lack of it—seems to be an epidemic among today's student population.

"Hi there, Tracy. What's your question for the doc?" Bill asks.

"Oh, well, actually, I don't really have a question. I just wanted to share some advice," she says, her voice cheerful and confident.

"All right then," Bill says. "Never hurts to get another perspective. What's your advice to our listeners?"

"I'm a university student, like your first caller. Actually, listening to Nikki's story is what inspired me to call in. It's such a relief to know that other students feel like group work is forcing them into weird late-night meetings. I was starting to think everyone had just become normalized to that sort of thing. So I wanted to share a system that's been working well for me in terms of coordinating members. Nikki, I hope you're still listening."

"Oh, I'm sure she is! Our listeners are famously loyal," Bill says with a light laugh.

Tracy laughs too and says, "That's truer than you know. I've been listening to your show for years, Bill."

"Is that right? Well then, by all means, let's hear what you've got to say."

"Okay. So here's the system. When it comes to coordinating meetings, I've found the earlier you organize things, the better. The best thing to do is schedule an initial group meeting as soon as the group is formed and the project assigned. This initial meeting really sets the pace of the meetings to come. During that first meeting, I like to brainstorm a road map of all the phases the project will have to go through. Then, based on these phases, we draw up a tentative schedule. Each team member gives times and dates when meetings won't work for them. These times are non-negotiable. For example, one classmate of mine was on the varsity soccer team and travelled most weekends for away games. That limited us to weekdays. My non-negotiable time was after ten-thirty at night."

"What happens after ten-thirty?" KC asks, thinking that this is an early bedtime for most university students.

"That's when my bedtime alarm goes off," she says.

"Bedtime alarm?" he asks, intrigued but confused.

"It's not like I go to sleep at ten-thirty. But that's when I start to unwind for the night so that I'm calm enough to actually fall asleep by about eleven-thirty."

"Tracy, this whole scenario sounds like a dream—no pun intended. Planning meetings early, establishing group consensus— all great ideas. But are your classmates always willing to do this?"

"Well, yeah. I mean, I am always dubbed the group granny. But I think because all the members of the group end up having their voices heard, people are into it. The trick is to establish this early. If you aren't organized with your meetings, you're inevitably going to run into scheduling conflicts. That's when the late-night cramming sessions start to creep in."

KC lets Tracy's advice sink in. Initially, he's surprised that her system works. After all, he can understand why many students would object to having their meeting times limited by the 10:30 p.m. cutoff. But he can also see the appeal of working with someone as highly organized as Tracy. Planning ahead means that group projects are prioritized before other events have a chance to pop up. It also ensures each group member is aware of how much time and effort will be involved in the project, preventing the common blunder of leaving most of the work till the day before it's due.

"Well, Tracy, I sincerely hope Nikki was listening!" he says. "You've given us all something to think about."

"You've also brought us right to the end of this segment, Tracy," Bill says, jumping in to wrap things up. "I'm afraid our hour with Dr. Kenneth Coghill is up. And it looks like it's come just in time, because let me tell you, faithful listeners, Kenneth is starting to look a little droopy here in the studio. I think we've wiped him out."

KC is about to protest this assessment or launch a clever retort, but then he takes a quick moment to check in with his energy levels, and he notices that it's true—he's started tilting toward tired. Hosting a radio show is still fairly new to him, and it's taxing work.

"Might be time to follow your own advice, Ken. Looks like you could use a nap."

"I won't argue with that, Bill."

"Wise man," Bill says with an air of self-satisfaction.

KC doesn't mind acknowledging a bit of late-afternoon fatigue, but that doesn't mean he's about to let Bill have the last word.

"I will say this, Bill. After an hour spent with you, a nap sounds like a beautiful thing."

CHAPTER 12

BASKETBALL WORLD CHAMPIONSHIPS

In this chapter, the team plays at the world championships in Turkey and learns firsthand about managing nerves, engaging in game-day prep and developing a personal energy management plan.

"So let me get this straight," Wanda says as she watches KC pack his suitcase. "You're going away yet again. For a couple of weeks yet again. And yet again, I don't know anything about it?"

KC turns to her with his eyebrows raised in protest. He's about to defend himself, but Wanda's eyes narrow in on him, and he gets the sense that the better course is to keep silent.

"And don't tell me you told me about this trip before," she says. "Because even if that's true, it won't be helpful at this moment."

KC travels a lot. He likes to joke that his habit of travel is why his marriage has lasted so long. The more he's away, the less she has to put up with him—and there's no way that can be a bad thing!

But Wanda doesn't always see things that way. Although they seem to argue more as they get older, KC's frequent absences aren't any easier than they ever were. Now that their children are grown, the empty house must feel even emptier when he's on the road.

KC knows he mentioned this trip weeks ago, maybe a month

ago. Part of him wants to dig in his heels and prove he's right. But another part of him—maybe the smarter part—remembers that being right doesn't necessarily help the relationship. Many years ago, he was in a workshop with Joan Borysenko. A single sentence she uttered in that workshop has stuck with him and changed his behaviour in situations like this one. She said, "You have to decide whether you want to be right or be happy."

Looking into his half-packed suitcase, KC once again considers this choice. He decides he wants to be happy, so he tries to diffuse his irritation with a few centring breaths. Wanda notices this effort and smiles. Then she sits down on the bed beside him.

"Where are you going this time?" she asks.

"The world basketball championships in Turkey," he replies.

"Okay, I do remember something about Turkey. But for some reason, I thought you were talking about Thanksgiving plans. Take an extra sweater at least," she says warmly. "It gets cold in Turkey this late in the fall."

His first day in Ankara, KC meets with the coaches at the sports complex. He stands courtside, next to Linda, the head coach, watching the players practice. The world championship is important, but it's not nearly as important as the Olympic Trials next summer. Because there's so much youth on the team, the coaches and KC agree that at this world championship, what's most important is development. The players need to get a lot better at competing, and competing requires exceptional energy management. Between now and Olympic Trials, they won't have a better development lab, so to speak, than this world championship. But nerves are running high.

"We've got some work ahead of us, Ken," Linda says.

"Well, let's hear it. What's your main concern going into this tournament?"

"I'm not sure how our players are going to handle the pressure— the younger ones especially. Take a look at Sarah, for example," she says, gesturing to the young point guard out on the court. "She really lets her nerves get the best of her. By the time she gets to the gym on game day, she's already been anxious for hours. In the first quarter of the game, she makes poor decisions, and she turns over the ball way too much. She's one of our quickest and most-talented players, but I really can't have her be a starter until she cleans that up. And she's not the only one, just the most-obvious example."

KC watches Sarah blaze down the court. She looks confident out there right now. But he'll have to find a way to help her retain that confidence under pressure. Last time KC was here, he talked to the players about how learning to compete in high-pressure situations is all about learning to use time and energy effectively. Every elite performer in any sphere needs an energy management game plan before important events, whether those be critical sales calls, major presentations or basketball games at the Olympic Trials. This time, he wants to get a clear idea of each player's attitude toward game day. He'll have a few group sessions with the team again, but he also wants one-on-one sessions with each of the players so that they can design individualized mental-preparation plans. Because everyone is different, their preparation plans will necessarily have to be different too. Of course, KC also understands that plans need to be adjusted, so after the first game, he'll meet with the players individually once more to adjust their personalized plans based on how effective those plans were on game day.

He lays out this strategy to Linda and the assistant coaches. Everyone agrees it's a good approach. But they also know that over the next few days, unexpected issues will arise to throw a wrench or two into the plan.

Indeed, the first wrench occurs near the end of the practice, when Rochelle comes down with a rebound onto the outside of Jessica's foot.

"Oww!" Rochelle howls. She follows this first scream of pain with a string of impressive expletives and then collapses onto the court, clutching her ankle.

A rush of coaches and players crowd around her and help her hobble off the court, where they usher her toward the team's medical doctor. After a quick exam, the doctor makes a diagnosis.

"It's a mild ankle sprain," she says. "It's going to take a bit of time to recover from this."

"Will I be able to play?" Rochelle asks, her eyes pleading for an affirmative response. "That's three days from now. I'll be fine in three days, right?"

"We'll have to see, Rochelle. But you've got to give this time to heal."

It's always rough to watch athletes get injured. They put so much work into their training, and one wonky landing can cause a deluge of disappointment. As KC watches Rochelle begin to process her diagnosis, he sees profound disappointment wash over her face. The coaches are also disappointed by this development. Rochelle's one of their better players, and now she's a question mark for the games. This is not the best start to the week.

The next morning, KC is up early. The first thing on his agenda is a session with the team, so after a quick breakfast at the hotel, he makes his way over to the sports complex and arrives just as the players do.

When all of the players are seated at the tables, KC starts. "This morning, I want to talk about competition days and how to manage your energy on those big-pressure days. So let's get right down to specifics. Your first game is Sunday against Brazil."

Brazil has always had a strong team, and their position as Olympic hosts in 2016 guarantees they'll be going all-out. There's no doubt Brazil is going to be a formidable opponent. It's a tough game to open with.

"Let's start with the night before the game," KC says. "What's the plan for Saturday night? Do any of you have some kind of ritual that helps you get to sleep on the night before the game?"

"I have a regular Saturday-night ritual. But I guess excessive alcohol consumption is out of the question in this case," Samantha says, ever the jokester.

"I know that you're joking, Sam, but since we're on the topic, let's talk a bit about this—about how lifestyle affects athletic performance."

KC describes how, many years ago, he heard John Underwood of the American Athletic Institute present some great information to the women's hockey team. John noted that when athletes have more than two drinks, it can disrupt the quality of their training for several days.

"No problem for me," Jessica says with a smile. "I don't go out drinking anyway. It just gets in the way of my Internet time."

The players laugh. Jessica has a reputation for being a homebody glued to her computer late into the night.

"Well, actually, I'm sorry to say that John Underwood also has a few words of advice for people like you, Jessica."

At this same presentation, John explained people have a common misconception that because using a computer isn't a physical activity, it allows them to unwind before bedtime and promotes rest and recovery. In reality, about 80 percent of the brain is involved in typical web-surfing activity, which doesn't allow for true rest or recovery at all.

"It's interesting when you think about it," KC says. "We spend so much time incorporating all the new science into our physical training, but we don't often look at the way our lifestyle habits detract from all that work."

"Well, that's the last time I crack a joke," says Samantha. "I had no idea I was going to lead us down this huge lifestyle rabbit hole."

This remark draws some further laughter from the players. Samantha often has that effect on the team.

"But it's an important rabbit hole to go down," KC says.

"Okay, but can we get back to the night before the game?" Monique asks.

"Yes, of course," KC says. "So to refresh your memories, I asked if any of you have rituals you do to help you fall asleep before a competition day."

"Don't mention drugs or alcohol," says Samantha, already giving up on her resolution not to crack any more jokes.

"Last time, you talked about the relaxation response," Jessica says. "I've been trying to do relaxation exercises on the night before a game. I guess it's sort of become a ritual. I've been using the exercise you describe on that *Inside Edge* CD. It really helps."

Samantha nods and says, "Yeah, I've used that a few times too." A sly smile appears on her face, and she can't help adding, "I love hearing your voice on that CD, Ken. You know, you have a terrific talent for putting women to sleep!"

"As that's the point of the exercise, I'll take that as a great compliment!" KC says, laughing.

"Look, my problem isn't falling asleep," says Sarah, bringing a more-serious note to the discussion. "But when I wake up on game day, well, that's when I realize I'm a nervous wreck, and given that the world championships only happen once every four years, I may never get to do another one of these. I feel like there's a lot of pressure on me."

"Okay, let's talk about that. I want to suggest that getting out of bed on game day requires a form of mindfulness. Just before you get up, I want you to notice how you're feeling and what you're thinking. Ideally, you want to get up with a smile on your face. You want to be looking forward to the day and the game. When that's not the case, when you aren't feeling ideal or when your chest is tight and you're feeling anxious, it's critical to notice how you're interpreting these signs of stress and maybe adjust those interpretations."

This is the perfect moment for KC to discuss some research about the relationship between perception and stressful situations. Interpreting bodily responses of stress in a positive light rather than a negative one might be a key to performing well when it most counts. An important figure in this research is Kelly McGonigal, a Stanford University psychologist whose mission in life is to make people happier and healthier. Kelly admits that for years, she instructed her patients to avoid stress. But now she's speaking out about the recent research that shows this avoidance has been the wrong approach all along. In her words, "the old understanding of stress as an unhelpful relic of our animal instincts is being replaced by the understanding that stress actually makes us socially smart— it's what allows us to be fully human."

The research makes it clear that when you change your mind about stress, you change your body's response to stress. The key is to change your mindset. For example, view an increase in heart rate and sweat production as your body preparing itself to meet a challenge. In other words, view these responses in a helpful way. Don't think of those symptoms as signs of anxiety. When you view symptoms as helpful, you prevent your blood vessels from constricting. Such constriction is one of the reasons chronic stress is typically related to cardiovascular disease. When you take on the mindset that stress can be helpful, then your blood vessels stay relaxed, and you minimize the drain on your energy.

KC knows he's dumping a lot of information on the players here, but they all seem interested in this line of discussion.

"I think I get it," says Jessica. "It's like when we work out. It's painful, but it's a good pain, because we're getting stronger as a result of the stress we're putting on our muscles."

"Except I don't know how much stronger I'm really getting," Sarah says glumly. "Especially when you look at those crazy squats Chris has us doing. Man, do they hurt. I could barely do one when I started. Now, a month later, I can only do four. Big whoopee!"

"That's three more squats than a month ago," KC says. "A three hundred percent improvement in thirty days is very impressive."

Sarah looks at him, unsure if he's toying with her or not. "It's pathetic, Ken. Most of the girls can do eight to ten. I've seen Rochelle do twelve—that's three times as many as me."

"Well, right now, I'm doing zero," Rochelle says with a nod at her ankle brace.

KC studies Sarah, whose disappointment in herself is plainly marked on her face. This is an issue he wants to address in his one-on-one conversation with her. Comparing herself to others is a major energy drain. They'll have to find ways to curb that tendency when they devise her individual game-day strategy. But that's an issue for their private meeting.

"Let's stay on track here," he says. "We were talking about getting out of bed on the day of the competition. So now you're out of bed and feeling positive about the day. How long will that last?"

"For me? Milliseconds," says Samantha. "Or until I run into a non–morning person like Jessica."

"Hey!" objects Jess. "Not everybody is Miss Congeniality first thing in the morning."

"Okay, what about the rest of the day?" says KC, hoping to break up their good-hearted squabbling before it steers the conversation off course. "How do your schedules break down on game day?"

Although their schedules vary depending on the competition, things basically follow this order: they have breakfast, shoot around, have lunch, nap, have a hotel meet-up, take a bus to the venue, do an individual off-court warm-up, put on uniforms, have an on-court warm-up, hold a dressing room talk, do on-floor intros and then, finally, face the opening tip-off.

"When you lay it out like that, it seems like a busy day," Monique says. "But actually, I always feel like time stretches on game day. I've got so much time to think—or agonize—about the upcoming game."

"One of the most-important things to do on game day is monitor your energy levels," KC says. "It's very easy to throw energy away by focusing on the game for the nine or ten hours before you actually have to play. That can physically exhaust you."

From a quick scan of the players' faces, he can see that this exhaustion is a reality most of them are well acquainted with.

Sharon is the first to jump in and share her thoughts on the matter. She says, "Oh my goodness, I so know what that's about. I remember when we had to play in the regional high-school final. I was so focused on that game all day long. It was all I thought about the whole day. And then, by the time I got to the gym, my legs felt like lead. I was so mentally exhausted at game time that I could barely care about the actual game. I mean, I did get into the game eventually. But it certainly wasn't one of my better games."

"I was doing that same thing a few years ago," Jessica says, eager to get in her two cents. "I was so uncomfortable all day because the game was front and centre in my mind. So I decided to go to a movie in the afternoon, hoping to distract myself from the game. It worked all right—too well. I was so into the movie that when I came out, I had trouble getting my head back in the game. I played a horrible first half."

Sharon and Jessica are two veteran players. For the younger players, who are especially overwhelmed by the pressure of big games, hearing these stories is invaluable.

"Those are great anecdotes," KC says. "Real examples that demonstrate why it's so important to touch base with yourself throughout the day. If your energy level is too high, bring it down. Try using the centring technique we discussed last time I was here."

As he looks at the group, he notices Keisha, one of the younger players, scrunching her brow in thought. Something's on her mind.

"Keisha? Something wrong?" he asks.

"Well, not really. It's just that I was thinking—what really gets into my head is imagining making a huge mistake during the game. Or really playing poorly. Those kinds of thoughts just pop into my head all day long. What am I supposed to do about that?"

KC begins, "Well, a good thing to do—"

However, Sharon breaks in. "I know just what you mean, Keisha. I totally used to do that all the time." She pauses, looking up, red-faced, at KC, realizing she's interrupted him.

"Don't let me stop you," KC says with a smile. "Carry on. When you've finished your career as a player, you'll probably be taking over the sport psychology role. So let's hear it. How did you deal with that sort of thing?"

Sharon's flush of embarrassment eases as she says, "Well, okay, so I don't know if this works for everybody, but when I notice myself imagining things like that, missing key shots, I stop and ask myself if that's what I want. And of course it's not. It's exactly what I *don't* want. So I replay the scenario in my mind, but when I do, I imagine doing it correctly, shooting a perfect shot with perfect form. I even imagine the smooth swish of the ball passing through the basket."

"But when do you do that kind of visualization?" says Keisha. "What if you're out with other people or in a line at the grocery store?"

"Ha! Sharon never goes to the grocery store on game day," Monique teases. "Have you seen her room, Keisha? She's so stocked with provisions you could feed a football team on what she's got stashed away. She's like a squirrel getting ready for winter."

"Is nothing sacred on this team?" Sharon asks with mock outrage. Then she turns to Keisha and says, "To answer your question, it really doesn't matter where I am, because I can make any corrections and visualize whatever I want without anyone noticing."

Monique starts laughing. "I don't think what you're doing is quite as subtle as you think, Sharon. Your visualizations don't always stay in your head. They usually bleed into real, physical action."

"Yeah, like that time we were standing in line for the breakfast buffet, and you startled three of us by taking a jump shot," Jess adds.

The women share a laugh at this memory—even Sharon gives in to the laughter.

KC loves when the players interject with their own stories and thoughts, but time is running short, and he needs to push on. "From my perspective as a sports psychologist, I love Sharon's methods of dealing with those little demons of doubt that creep up on game day. You've heard me say many times that imagery is the language of performance."

"Thank you, KC. I'm glad someone appreciates my efforts," Sharon says.

"And I hope you'll all appreciate my efforts to keep this conversation moving along. We've been working our way through game day, discussing how important it is to monitor energy levels and keep your thoughts from straying to the negative. Now it's almost game time—one hour to tip-off. What happens during the warm-up before the game?"

"Stretching mostly," says Samantha, smiling.

"And nerves," adds Sarah. "It's in the warm-up that my nerves really start to get out of control."

"A clear plan for your warm-up hour will really help with those nerves, Sarah," KC says.

"What kind of plan?"

"Well, during a warm-up, it's important to remember that you don't just need to warm up your body. You need to warm up your mind as well. And that means focus. If, for example, you're stretching and you're busy talking to one of your teammates, then you aren't totally focusing on the stretches. You're not developing that narrow focus you need during the game. So in the warm-up, stay focused. Don't distract yourself with idle chatter, and don't worry about what might happen during the game. Just focus on what is happening and how your body is stretching. That's the habit you want to get into."

"I had another thought about warm-up time," Monique says. "I just feel like it's easy to waste a lot of energy in that hour. It's easy to get caught up showing off for the crowd, thinking about the opposing team, or worrying about the game ahead. There's just so much energy in the arena in that pregame hour—it's so easy to get swept up in it. But really, the time to get amped up to game intensity is maybe five minutes before tip-off, not earlier."

"That's well put, Monique. It's crucial to save your energy for the game. How many of you know who Al McGuire was?" KC asks.

Not a single hand in the room goes up, reminding KC once again of the tremendous age difference between him and the players. But he continues with his story of Al, the basketball coach at Marquette in the seventies, back when KC was coaching basketball. Al once told KC that his philosophy of basketball was based on his father's bar in Chicago. The bar was on a commuter line and got a lot of after-work traffic. One day, Al's father figured out that he made more money if he took all of the seats out of the bar and made the patrons stand. It seemed like an odd idea at first, but his father had noticed that patrons ordered a drink or two and then just hung around in the comfy chairs, taking up space that would be more profitable if occupied by new patrons willing to order their own drink or two. The business would be more successful if he could get people in quickly and out just as quickly. Al carried that thinking over to coaching basketball.

"Al believed that basketball games were won in the first three minutes of the game, the last three minutes of the first half, the first three minutes of the second half and the last three minutes of the game," KC tells the players. "So Al did everything he could to energize his players for those four time frames. Marquette was the first school to go through elaborate pregame introductions with the lights dimmed in the arena, and sometimes Al took intentional technical fouls to energize his team at key moments. He was a one-of-a-kind coach in a very different era, but he sure understood the importance of energy at key moments in the game."

"I like the sound of this guy!" says Samantha.

"Oh yeah, he was a great guy. Real solid guy." As KC's mind wanders down memory lane, he indulges in some of the funniest stories about Coach McGuire. There's a great one about the challenges he faced while recruiting at Marquette. Al knew there were certain players he couldn't possibly get to come to Marquette, so he sent out negative recruiting letters to those players—top-prospect players—telling them that he was sorry, but he didn't have room for them at Marquette. "Way I figure it is, somewhere down the line, I'm helping one of my coaching buddies deal with the massive egos of the high draft picks," he told KC once, chuckling.

As KC relates these old stories to the players, the whole team is laughing and hanging on his every word—the storyteller in him is on a roll. But when a look at the time shows him the session is almost up, he realizes he might have gotten a bit carried away.

"Okay, okay, enough of Coach McGuire for the moment. Let's talk about how to manage energy once the game starts. My advice here is really pretty simple. Don't spend a lot of time in your head. Stay in the game; stay out there. Stay engaged in what's happening on the court."

"This is advice I can get behind," says Samantha. "Only bad things happen when I spend too much time in my head."

"That's true of your head especially, Sam," KC teases. "But seriously, if you see someone make a mistake, take a minute to slip inside your head and imagine how you would have played that scenario correctly. It's best to mentally edit those negative film clips. But once you've corrected the minimovie in your head, get back out there with the rest of us! Same thing goes during halftime. There's no point spending that time analyzing everything you could've done better in the first half. Just ask yourself this: What is the one thing you want to do better in the second half? Think about that on Sunday when you're playing Brazil."

The game against Brazil turns out to be tougher than expected. It's a decisive loss for the team, but it's also a learning opportunity. These tough games help the players develop their skills—the particular skills they'll need at Olympic Trials next summer. The primary goal of the coaching staff is for the team to qualify for the quarterfinals. If they achieve this goal, they'll get the experience of playing at least three more highly competitive games against highly competitive teams. That's invaluable experience. KC refers to this process as "going to school." But the game against Brazil was a tough education.

On Monday morning, KC is up early to meet with the coaches—Linda, Sean and Wendy.

"Morning, Linda," he says, approaching the team breakfast table. All three of the coaches are already seated for breakfast. The coaches always arrive about 15 minutes before the players do. The extra time allows them to talk about key issues.

"Good morning, Kenneth," replies Linda. "Still think last night was just 'going to school'?"

"School of hard knocks," says Sean. "I don't think some of our younger players know what hit them. Brazil is a physically tough team, and our younger players just aren't used to that much contact under the basket."

"They do have a lot to learn," says Wendy. "But I thought they played with more grit and sandpaper in the second half. If they can keep up that level of play against Mozambique tonight, we'll be just fine."

This is something they knew coming in: their must-win game is the one against Mozambique. The competition is broken up into four pools, each made up of four teams. The top team in each of these pools automatically qualifies for the quarterfinals. The bottom team in each pool goes home. The second- and third-place teams in each pool play crossover games against a team from another pool, and the winners of those games also qualify for the quarterfinals.

"I agree, Wendy," says Sean. "All we need is to win at least one game in our pool. That game is tonight—Mozambique."

"The education continues," says KC, smiling as he takes his first sip of coffee.

After breakfast, KC meets with the players individually to go over their personalized energy management plans. In light of each player's performance in the Brazil game, they try to determine how effective those plans have been—what served them well and what didn't. From there, they modify the plans accordingly. It takes constant tweaking, but after working his way through the entire team, KC feels good about the results.

Next up on the day's agenda is a brief session with the team as whole.

"I just want to do a quick exercise today," he says. "So pick a partner."

The players waste no time in partnering up, and in less than a minute, KC sees six teams of two, all of whom are looking at him expectantly.

"Good. Now I want you to tell your partner one thing that you want to do better in the game tonight—something you want to do better than you did last night."

Soon there room is abuzz with conversation. One of the best things about athletes is that they're aware of their shortcomings. It doesn't take much prompting for these women to identify where they lagged last night and where they want to improve.

When the sounds of eager conversation seem to taper off slightly, KC moves to the next phase of the exercise. "Now we'll take turns sharing with the team. I want each of you to tell the team the one thing your partner is hoping to do better tonight."

Having to repeat what their partners told them is a great way to determine how well they've listened to each other. Coach K, at Duke University, once pointed out that there are three systems in basketball: the offensive system, the defensive system and the communication system. Without that last system, nothing works.

Once each of the players has shared her partner's personal-improvement goal for tonight's game, KC brings the session to a close. The players migrate out of the room, back to their hotel rooms for a nap or out for a walk—whatever they need to get them to their ideal energy level for the game. As KC gathers his things, he notices that two players have hung back. Monique and Samantha are waiting to talk to him.

"KC," says Monique, "can we get your input on something?"

"Well, sure. Anything."

"It's about meditation. I know you've talked about this before, but I've never actually tried it. And now it seems like everyone from Oprah to my mother is promoting it. So I guess I'm wondering—"

"*We* are wondering," corrects Samantha.

"Right. We are wondering—is it really that good for you?"

KC is thrilled to see these players displaying an interest in the practice. "Look, this is just my opinion, but there's nothing you could do for yourself that would serve you so well for the rest of your life. Meditation is a remarkable practice."

"Will it help our game?"

"It'll help every aspect of your life. That's my opinion at least."

"But what's so great about it?" Samantha asks. "I'm not sure I really get the point."

"Meditation has two facets. One is awareness, or learning to focus on what's happening now, in the present. The other is acceptance, or learning to accept your thoughts and emotions instead of simply reacting to them. Both can have a profound effect on your thinking, your attitude and your outlook."

Samantha nods but seems uncertain. Her expression is serious for a change; she's laid the jokes aside. KC loves the humour she brings to the team, but it's good to see this side of her too.

"What's going on in that head of yours, Sam?" he asks.

"It's just that I don't really know how to go about it—like how to get started. I feel like I should read a few books or something."

"I read for years about meditation, Sam—tons of books—and I attended tons of lectures on the subject. It was all very interesting and thought-provoking. Did you know that almost every religion has a sect that practices meditation? Not that that makes meditation a religious exercise—it's just interesting to think about. Meditation is centuries old. But sometimes it seems as if it was developed for our time, when you think of the speed and complexity of our world and the constant overload we experience. Anyway, I finally stopped reading about meditation altogether."

"Why?" they ask simultaneously, their expressions united in confusion.

"Think of it like this: you might read about an interesting place, and your friends might describe that place to you, but until you personally physically go there, you really don't know what it's like. Same thing with meditation. You have to practice it—do it, not just fantasize about it."

"Okay, but I really don't know where to start. I get that it's important to actually practice it, but aren't there a few good books we should read?" Samantha asks.

"Oh, I didn't mean to imply that you shouldn't read anything. I was just pointing out that I got so caught up in the reading that for a long time, I neglected the practice. Read to understand, but practice to develop. There are plenty of excellent books. I'll bring a few that might interest the two of you."

"Thanks, KC."

"And now, seeing as we're talking about awareness, I'm aware that there's somewhere you two need to get to—and in a hurry."

"Chalk talk with the coaches!" they yell in unison, and they sprint out the door.

That night, the team steps up their game. Their energy on the court is much better than it was the night before, especially on the offensive side of things. But in spite of that improvement, they're still down by two points at the half.

KC walks into the dressing room to find Linda giving the team her halftime talk. She's direct in her message: the players need to increase their level of energy on defence.

"There's way too much switching going on when they set a screen," Linda says. "You need to fight over the top of that screen. Or if your player is doing the screening, you need to communicate very early with your teammate—step back and pull her behind the screen. Either way, we need to stop switching, because we're creating mismatches. Our small players end up on their big players and vice versa, and that's causing us all kinds of problems."

"We're being too tentative at both ends of the floor," Sean adds. "We're making the very mistakes that we fear. If we increase our energy on defence, it'll transfer to the offensive side of things. We'll score more baskets. It's that simple."

The players nod; they agree. When they get back on the court for the second half, they put this strategy into action. They bump up their energy on defence. They communicate more fluidly and effectively. They play in sync. By the end of the third quarter, they're up by 12. At the final buzzer, they've pulled away to an 18-point lead. It's exactly the kind of win they wanted to achieve.

In the locker room after their win, the team debriefs the game. They use a procedure that KC helped them develop in an earlier session: Prior to the game, the players come up with a list of questions to ask themselves during the debriefing. They then discuss these questions after the game, before the coaches weigh in with their thoughts and suggestions. The idea feeds into the going-to-school process. The ultimate goal in any coaching situation is to build self-awareness and self-responsibility.

Allowing the players to debrief their own game also gives the coaches a glimpse into the players' minds. It's clear from tonight's discussion that the players have not only learned a lot from their tough game against Brazil but also applied those learnings in the second half.

They've made tremendous progress. Already, KC is looking forward to seeing how much further this team can go.

As the tournament proceeds, the team gets better and better. Although they don't win every game, their performance is on an upward trajectory. In their next game, they meet host country Turkey and play in front of a full house packed with noisy fans—it's a 10-point loss for the team. Two days later, they're matched up against France, the number-two-ranked team in the world. They give France a run for its money, losing by just two points. In a crossover game, they run into the Czech Republic and win decisively.

The team makes it into the quarterfinals, just as they hoped. In this round, they lose to a good Australian team but bounce back to win their final games. All in all, the coaches are thrilled with the tournament and the development of the players. The team went in ranked ninth in the world and came out ranked fifth. But more important than this great upward climb are the many vital lessons they learned throughout. Things are looking up for the Olympic Trials next summer.

On the last night before he leaves, KC has trouble falling asleep. His mind is racing with thoughts about the players, and he wonders about all of the things he might not have covered. History has taught him that it's often in the quiet before sleep that he unexpectedly hits on some of his best ideas. As he lies in bed, his mind churns things over—things he's long stopped thinking about, at least on the conscious level. Mark Fenske, a brain researcher, once spoke to KC and a few other sports-psych types about this phenomenon. Mark explained that many of our best ideas come when the brain isn't preoccupied with what we're doing, when it's free to be creative—such as in the shower or in bed late at night.

Since that conversation, KC has taken to capturing these late-night thoughts and off-loading them onto a reliable memory platform. Sometimes he jots them down on a piece of paper, and other times he dictates them into his iPhone. He used to think he'd just remember his ideas, but as they consistently evaporated in the morning, he began to learn his lesson. Now his mind doesn't trust that he'll remember the ideas, so if he doesn't write them down, his mind repeats them over and over and sometimes starts to develop and expand the ideas, keeping KC wide awake. It takes a just a few minutes to capture them, an effort that lets his mind relax and lets sleep sweep in.

Tonight he jots down an idea he has for tomorrow's group session. Then he flicks off the light and drifts into a deep sleep.

In the morning, KC looks at the notepad on his bedside table and sees the words *Noble Cause* scribbled on the page. He first learned about the Our Noble Cause exercise from a book called *Tribal Leadership* by Dave Logan, John King and Halee Fischer-Wright. It's an exercise he wants to do with the basketball team—not at this tournament but at training camp before the Olympic Trials next summer.

In terms of energizing, there's nothing as effective as having a clear sense of purpose, a vision. To find an excellent example of this, KC has to look no further than his own parents, both of whom embodied the power of purpose, as did many parents in the post–World War II era. KC's father, a Danish immigrant, came to Canada in the hopes of finding a better life. He worked in a mine for 42 years, underground all those years, excepting the five-year break when he was overseas with the Allied forces in the war. When he returned from the war, boy, did he have a clear sense of purpose. He made sure all four of his children would have a better life than he'd had, that they'd be well educated. KC often thinks that maybe his father was able to tolerate the backbreaking labour in that harsh, underground environment for all those decades because of his clear sense of purpose. KC's father knew why he did what he did.

It's the bigger things in life that provide exceptional motivation and energy. Sometimes we have to ensure that we bring these things into our lives. The Our Noble Cause exercise is a small attempt to do this in a meaningful way. He did this exercise with the Canadian women's hockey team just before the Sochi Olympics.

The team was training just outside of Vienna for 10 days prior to going to Sochi. After practice one day, in his team session, he asked them what their goal was for the Olympic Games.

"To win gold!" they all exclaimed.

"But in service of what? For what purpose?" he asked them.

The players then discussed their noble cause—their raison d'être, their reason for being. They brainstormed thoughts and ideas, writing everything down on some chart paper, and eventually, three themes emerged. From these themes, KC wrote out a rough draft of their noble cause. It underwent several editorial revisions, but eventually, the whole team agreed on the wording, and then they had it handwritten on three canvas panels.

The first panel read, "The game is in us."

The second panel read, "We do what we do to the highest standard while inspiring and unifying Canadians and honouring all the many who have supported and believed in us."

The final panel read, "We accept that adversity comes with the pursuit of excellence, and it unites us as a team."

That team won Olympic gold.

CHAPTER 13

OPTIMAL IT TURNS THE CORNER

In this chapter, we learn about an energizing substitution at Optimal IT, a happiness decision by Marcel and his wife and the ways we make ourselves unhappy—even though we definitely don't want to be.

Alone at home, KC spends the day doing chores around the house— replacing a few lightbulbs, raking some leaves and pruning the bushes. Every time he gets back from a trip, it seems as if a dozen chores have popped up in his absence.

He's alone today because Wanda has gone on a trip of her own, out west for a visit with their grandchildren. She left the day after he returned from Istanbul—but not before she let him know he has to start cutting back on work and making more time for family.

"It'd be nice if our grandchildren actually knew who you were!" she said.

That line has been replaying in KC's head all day. He had a great time in Turkey, but here at home, in his own life, he's not spending as much time as he should on the bigger things. He needs to focus on his own noble cause.

"She's right," he says to himself as he unscrews a burnt-out light bulb in the kitchen. "I have to start making time for the family, for the grandkids. They'll be grown before I know it."

Once he gets the new bulb in place, he feels his iPhone buzz with a text. It's Karen, asking him to meet up bright and early Monday morning for an eight o'clock breakfast meeting at their usual spot.

KC fires off a quick affirmative reply and then gets back to puttering around the house.

On Monday at seven-thirty, KC walks into the lobby of the Crestwood Inn. He purposely arrives a bit early, thinking he can spend the extra half hour collecting his thoughts on the Optimal IT–related issues. But he has no such luck, as Karen's already here. She's sitting at their usual table with an upbeat air about her. He's pleased to see her in this mood—the last time he saw her, she was still fuming about her fight with her sister.

"You're looking awfully chipper this morning," he says, taking a seat opposite her. "How are things with your sister, Kathy?"

At once, Karen's expression darkens. "I haven't seen you in almost two weeks, because you've been doing very important things, like putting air into basketballs, and you open by mentioning Kathy," she chides. "You really aren't interested in having an amicable relationship with me, are you? That's like asking Dominic about Henri before even offering up a *good morning.*"

"I'll take that to mean things with your sister are still the same. And that you're still upset that I get to go away and work with eager athletes while you're stuck here facing the Henri challenge."

"I might be a little upset about the unfairness of that, yes," she says, tweaking the corners of her mouth into a smile.

"Well then, I'll spare you the tales of my truly excellent trip," he says with a grin of his own. "But speaking of our favourite HR challenge, how has Henri been this week?"

Karen's eyes twinkle as she sips her coffee. "Henri?" she says casually. "Oh, he's gone. I thought I told you about that in an e-mail. Did I neglect to mention that?"

The wheels in KC's brain start to turn. He knows Karen would never lie to him, but Henri is gone? Can that be? "Uh ..."

"Yes, Henri is gone. Well, at least for a week."

"Oh. So he took a week off? Vacation?"

"Not exactly, although it sure feels like the rest of the team has been on a vacation this past week. With Henri out of the office, it's been smooth sailing."

"But wait. I don't follow. If he's not on vacation and not at the office, where is he?"

"I sent him on a one-week program called Attitude Delivers Results. It's supposed to help him learn the importance of a good attitude."

"I can't imagine he was too keen on that idea," KC says.

"No. No, he wasn't," Karen says.

Karen is quiet for a moment, but KC wants a more-extensive explanation of this surprising development with Henri. He fixes an expectant look on her until she offers up a few more details. She explains how she sat down Henri and made it clear that the program was mandatory. She told him that if he were to stay on at Optimal IT, he needed an attitude adjustment. There was no discussion. To fill in for Henri during his absence, she hired a consultant, Marcel. The result has been a week of progress, learning and workplace bliss.

"Marcel's been great. He fit in right away. He knows a ton about encryption, and he loves to teach, so everyone feels like they've learned a lot this week. The energy has been incredible."

"This is terrific, Karen!" says KC.

"Yeah. The only problem is that the program is just a week," Karen says. She checks her watch and adds, "So in about an hour, Henri returns."

Just then, over Karen's shoulder, KC spots a familiar face enter the lobby of the hotel. It's Dominic, standing there in the lobby, looking around, searching for someone. Karen follows KC's gaze, and when she sees Dominic, she says, "Oh yeah. That's right. I asked Dominic to join us this morning. I thought it might be a good idea."

Karen turns to face the lobby and, with a big wave, catches Dominic's attention. He hurries over to join them at their table, offering up quick greetings to both of them. As he slides into his seat, a server comes over to take their orders: soft-boiled eggs and toast for Karen and Dominic and muesli for KC—light fare all around.

"Karen was just telling me about your week without Henri," KC says after the server has gone. "How's it been?"

Dominic looks up at the ceiling, trying to find the right words to describe his Henri-less week. "Ever been at a party where someone leaves, and it feels like someone really nice just came in?" he says at last.

"Yes. I know just the feeling."

"That's how it's been without Henri. Things have really turned around. There are still some challenges, of course, but we're on task, particularly with our new client. The plan we put together in our last session has worked well, Ken. And you know, I can really tell that the team is focusing on their energy management."

"How can you tell?" asks Karen eagerly. "Are your people telling you about any energy management changes they've implemented? If so, I'd love that list, because we really want to take this program company-wide, and any examples of its success will help me convince Douglas."

Dominic shrugs and says cryptically, "It's the recycling bin."

KC and Karen exchange puzzled looks. "Recycling bin?" they ask together.

"Right. The recycling bin," says Dominic with an uncharacteristic glint in his eye. "You know, now that I think about it, I can't believe I didn't see the energy problem sooner. I mean, it was just so obvious, right there in all those empty cans of Red Bull and 5-Hour Energy and piles of Starbucks cups. These things are like the canary in the coal mine. They're signs that the team lacks energy from midday on. This past week, the recycling-bin pile was down by about sixty percent. People are finding healthier ways to recharge their batteries. They're taking those energy breaks. They're getting their rest."

"The recycling bin," Karen says, laughing loudly. "How obvious! You know, Ken, Dominic here has just given you a great idea for finding potential clients."

"I know where you're going with that, Karen, but I'm not about to become a Dumpster diver," KC says.

"With that kind of narrow-minded research orientation, it's a wonder you have any clients at all!"

The return of their server, who arrives with small plates of simple but delicious food, interrupts their laughter. As breakfast gets underway, KC gets the conversation back on task.

"So, Dominic, overall, how are things going for you?"

Between bites of his toast, Dominic explains that on a personal level, things have improved for him. His own energy levels have been up because he's made more of an effort to consider how he manages that energy. But he admits that the impending return of Henri has been weighing on him. Frankly, he's been dreading it.

"Henri's a bright guy, and he knows why he was sent away on this program," Dominic says. "I've heard that this program is downright transformational for some people. So I don't know—I guess I'm really hoping Henri is one of those people."

"We'll find out shortly," says Karen.

"So we're still on for our nine o'clock meeting with Henri then?" he asks.

"We are."

Dominic dabs at his face with his napkin as he finishes the last of his eggs. "Great. We should maybe get going."

"Oh, I guess that's true. Time's a-ticking," says Karen. Then she looks over at KC. "But I had a few more things to discuss with you, Mr. Jet-Setter. What do you say—want to come over to the office? It's not Istanbul, but we have finished up with the construction now. I think you'll like it. It feels peaceful over there again, and there are some great views of the woods."

"How could I say no?" KC asks.

Wandering through the corridors of Optimal IT, KC marvels at the changes around the place. The renovations are terrific, and the office looks amazing—sleek, clean and modern but warm and friendly. Large windows everywhere let in soft light, and the views of the woods outside have a calming effect on KC. He stands at one end of a hallway, happily lost in thought, gazing through the window at the maple trees, while he waits for Karen to conclude her meeting with Dominic and Henri.

As it turns out, he doesn't have to wait long. Before he has time to sink into a nature-inspired reverie, he hears a door open and turns to see Karen and Dominic come out of a meeting room to confer between themselves in the hallway.

"Done already?" KC asks, approaching them.

"There wasn't much to discuss," Karen says with a heavy sigh. "We asked him how the program went, and he just sat there, rolling his eyes. He said there wasn't anything at all for him to learn, that it was a waste of time."

Dominic shakes his head, his eyes downcast. "I was really hoping the program would help him. There must be something else we can do here."

Karen looks him right in the eye and says, "Dominic, you've done everything you could possibly do here. You've tried to coach Henri into being a more-serviceable member of your high-performance team. He's got the skills, sure. But, well, to put it bluntly, Henri isn't coachable."

"But how can you be so sure? Maybe I haven't tried the right things. Maybe somebody else would be better able to coach him."

Karen takes a deep breath and takes a step closer to Dominic. "I believe very strongly in people's ability to change. But there are some people who need to *want* to change themselves first. There are some people who, with all due respect, don't need coaching. They need therapy."

Dominic opens his mouth as if to say something but closes it again before any words come out.

Karen continues, "Martin Seligman, at the University of Pennsylvania, talked about the three Ps that are associated with uncoachable people: personal, permanent and pervasive. Personal in the sense that the behaviour is part of who they are, permanent in the sense that it's how they've always been, and pervasive in the sense that you can see the behaviour in every environment the person is in. When you see a behaviour in someone that's personal, permanent and pervasive, you're not going to be able to coach a change in that behaviour. Henri's behaviour captures all three Ps. You and I, Dominic, do not have the skills to effect a change in Henri. What we can do is try to give him the support he needs by way of our employee-assistance program. We need to do this for his sake. But just as importantly, we need to consider all the other people who have to work with him."

"I guess I can see that," says Dominic after a long, thoughtful pause. "It was just so evident last week. Everybody got so much work done, and I know that's because they weren't spending all their time and energy adjusting to him. So what's our next step?"

"Henri has to go," says Karen matter-of-factly.

"Okay. I agree," says Dominic, relieved now that the decision has been made. But the practical concerns cause some tension to linger in him. "What about Henri's expertise, though? Do you think Marcel might be available to help us for a few weeks?"

"I happen to know that he is. I spoke to him on Friday, and he said he could join us as early as tomorrow if we need him."

At this bit of information, the last dregs of tension in Dominic seem to evaporate. His shoulders drop, his expression relaxes and he exclaims, "I could just hug you! I don't know how I'd have gotten through this without you. And without Kenneth." With these last words, he looks at KC and offers a grateful nod.

KC responds with a nod of his own, but he keeps quiet. Karen seems to be handling the situation marvellously.

"So what should I do now?" Dominic asks.

"You need to get to back to work with your team," she says. "I'll be dealing with Henri. You'll just need to keep this quiet until we make a formal announcement." There's a short moment of quiet while they each reflect on this significant decision. Then Karen breaks into a smile and adds, "I'll take that hug now!"

Over the next few weeks, the change in Dominic's department is nothing short of transformational. Marcel is every bit as helpful as he was in his first week with the department, and his presence allows the team to finally gel and to grow. After months of struggling, they're finally on a good, clear path. They even manage to get ahead on the Metronome project.

In the wake of this progress, Karen pushes for the energy management program to go company-wide. Faced with the cold, hard proof of success, Douglas welcomes the expansion of the program. Soon KC and Karen are rolling out the program from one department to the next, offering one workshop after another, with an aim to get the whole company aboard.

Everything seems to be going well, so KC is alarmed when, early one morning, he gets an e-mail from Karen that reads,

> Need some help re: an issue I'm having with
> Marcel.
> Call me.

He calls Karen immediately, and as soon as she picks up, he says, "What's the issue with Marcel? I thought he was fitting in really well."

"And a good afternoon to you too, Ken. How are you doing?"

Even though he's a few miles away, he has no trouble visualizing her smirk as she chides him for his poor phone decorum.

"Ah, I'm fine, Karen. Forgive me for my lack of social graces. I was just shocked to hear things weren't going well with Marcel."

"I'd be shocked too if I heard things weren't going well with Marcel. But Marcel's a dream. What makes you think he's trouble?"

"Well, your e-mail suggested ..." KC stammers.

"I said I had an issue with him. And the issue is that he's incredibly talented and incredibly well liked. So—"

"And that's an issue for you because?" KC says, interrupting.

"If you'd let me finish, I'd tell you," says Karen. "It's an issue because he's on contract, and that contract is just about up. Douglas, you remember your golfing buddy; he doesn't want us reliant on consultants. He wants the entire team to be full-time employees. And we can't do without Marcel at the moment."

She pauses, but KC is wisely wary of interrupting her a second time. He waits for a moment to see if she has more to add, and sure enough, after this brief pause to take a breath, Karen picks back up.

"Now, I met with Marcel twice last week. He's really enjoying his work here. But he makes more money as a consultant than we can pay him as a full-time employee. He'd get an excellent benefit package here, but it's still short of the financial package he currently has. So that's where we're at. I thought you might be able to help."

"Well, as long as you're not planning on redirecting some of my fee toward boosting his salary," he teases.

"Oh, I thought about that. I mean, when I consider how amazingly competent he is and how you just seem to float around, making casual appearances at easily facilitated workshops," she jokes. "But seriously, I thought you might be able to help him reframe the benefits of staying here. I can think of a few advantages for him off the top of my head. I know he has to travel a lot as a consultant, for one. He hates that. He's got a young family and would much prefer to be closer to home. I remember you talking to me about some book—*Joyful Money*, I think it was called—and I thought there might be something in that that might induce Marcel to stay."

"I think you mean *Happy Money* by Elizabeth Dunn and Michael Norton."

"That's right. Happy, joyful—same thing, right?"

"Well, not exactly. But okay. If Marcel is willing, I'd be glad to sit down with him to help him flush out what's best for him. And if that happens to be good for Optimal IT, then great! But you need to understand that if I'm going to meet with him, it'll be under the same conditions as I meet with the athletes. I'm in their corner, and what gets said stays between us—between Marcel and me."

"Fine by me. I don't want to force anyone into a situation that isn't good for him. I just think that there's always more to the picture than money. And as far as him being willing, it was actually he who suggested it! He loved the workshop you did with the team last week, and he's a bit of a sports nut, so he loves the idea of having a chat with—as he put it—'a well-recognized sports psychologist.' I'd have used other adjectives to describe you, but I kept them to myself," she jokes.

"That's new! It's a great sign of personal growth on your part to be able to withhold a correction. I'm sure you were going to describe me as world famous, weren't you?"

"Precisely. But even then, I'd have hated to limit my description of your skills to just this world, this planet, because sometimes your skills are really universal. By that, I mean out there in space."

KC laughs and says, "Tell Marcel I'll talk to him this afternoon."

"Thanks, Ken."

Later that day, KC meets with Marcel in his office. Marcel isn't just good at his job; he's easy to be around and a good guy. His gentle eyes and warm smile put people at ease. It's no wonder Karen is eager to keep a hold of him. Within just a few minutes of conversation, it's clear to KC that the feeling is mutual. Marcel likes the work he's doing at Optimal IT, and he likes the team.

"I know this is a tough decision for you and your wife," KC says to him. "But it's good to know you're in demand. I'm not here to convince you one way or the other, but I want to make sure you're looking at the whole picture when you're making your decision."

"What exactly do you mean by the 'whole picture'?"

"I just think you owe it to yourself and your family to look at the situation from more than a financial perspective. I suspect, like most of us, you and your wife just want to maximize what you're getting out of this opportunity. I know this sounds corny, but I'm sure you just want to be happy. It's so obvious, and yet this is something that often gets left out of our decision making."

"Our personal happiness?"

"Right."

"But how do Sandy—that's my wife—and I go about looking at the bigger framework? Would you be willing to meet with us?"

"Sure. I'm more than willing to do that, if you like. You like to read, right? And your wife, Sandy—is she an avid reader?"

"Uh, yes, she is. Why?"

KC laughs at this bit of confusion he's wrought in Marcel. "Sorry for that sharp conversational turn there. People who know me get used to those. It's just that there's a book that summarizes all of this much better than I ever could. It'd be a great resource for you both to look at before making your decision." KC reaches into his bag and pulls out two copies of *Happy Money*, both of which he offers to Marcel. "I took the liberty of getting both you and your wife a copy, so you can read it at the same time. You've only got ten days to make this decision—not a lot of time."

"No, we're really under the gun. And it's still pretty busy here during the week, so I'm not even sure when my wife and I will be able to meet with you!" he says, laughing at the logistical trouble.

"A weekday meeting might be a bit tricky—that's true. What about Saturday? Are you available then?"

"Oh, that'd be great, Kenneth. At least I think so." Marcel laughs again, just a short, soft chuckle. "I have to be honest here— Sandy's the one who organizes our weekend schedule, so I can't tell you when we're free!"

"Check with the missus. Then let me know."

That night, KC gets a text from Marcel, asking if they can meet at ten o'clock on Saturday morning. As it happens, Marcel's two children have a soccer game that runs from ten o'clock to eleven o'clock, and they schedule the meeting to take place at a picnic table off to the side of the soccer pitch.

An outdoor meeting! KC is eager to agree.

KC's wife, however, isn't thrilled to find out he's made a commitment for a Saturday morning. She's even less impressed when she finds out it's to help another couple figure out how to find happiness.

"It's not just about their domestic happiness," KC pleads. "This is about my consulting work at Optimal IT. And I'm trying to help these people make a good decision—a big decision."

"I applaud your efforts to help others. But what about actually applying some of this stuff here at home? I've never even heard of this book *Happy Money*. You've never mentioned it to me. It's always the cobbler who wears the worst shoes."

KC has nothing to say. He knows she's right.

"I think it's time we took a careful look at our own lives," Wanda continues. "At your schedule in particular. And at what we want heading into the future."

"You're absolutely right, Wanda," KC says with sincerity. "We need to sit down and get a sense of where we're going and what we want to get out of our lives. It's just, well, you know how much I enjoy my work. I don't want to suddenly retire. I'd like to cut back slowly, if that's possible."

"I have no intention of stopping you from doing what you love. But we need to come up with a better balance, Kenneth."

KC knows this request is not unreasonable. He needs to do a better job of applying his advice to his own life with his own wife.

"Let's sit down at the end of the weekend and talk it over," he says, resting a hand on her shoulder. "We'll come up with some kind of plan."

"I'm going to hold you to that," she says.

Saturday turns out to be a beautiful day—so beautiful, in fact, that KC dusts off Mighty Mouse, his vintage MGB. It's the fourth time he's taken her out in the last two months.

"Bound and determined to use your *baby* more than five times this year just to prove me wrong, aren't you?" says Wanda as he's turning the ignition.

KC revs the engine, pretending not to hear her.

"I know you heard me, Ken!" she says, and she laughs at his childish attempt to evade a losing argument.

She's often maddeningly right. The truth is, he didn't want to go to the trouble of taking the tarp off of the car for such a short trip. However, to save face, he revs the engine once more and then pulls the car out of the driveway and gets on his way without further engaging in the discussion.

The soccer field is adjacent to a high school, and as KC pulls into the school parking lot, he sees four athletic-looking teenage boys clustered by the curb.

"Now, that's a cool car," one of them says. "What is it?"

"MGB," replies KC as he gets out of the car, delighted to see his baby getting some attention.

Judging by the blank looks on their faces, he might as well have said a Martian spaceship.

"Whatever," says the biggest of the group, a big, burly rugby-playing type. "It's a neat little car, but I doubt I'd even fit in it. My girlfriend would love it, though. She loves cute."

KC frowns. *Cute* isn't the adjective that's supposed to come to mind here.

"Hey, Ken!" someone calls.

Looking around, KC spots Marcel waving to him from the soccer field with a woman—presumably his wife—by his side. KC breathes out a sigh of relief, glad to escape further car talk with the teenagers. But as he approaches the pair, the woman eyes KC's car and cries out, "Oh! My goodness. Marcel, look at that cute Barbie car. I love it!"

Marcel turns on her with a stern expression. "Sandy, that's a vintage MGB. It's an iconic car. I'd kill to find one in mint condition like this one."

KC has two thoughts. The first is *I like Marcel even more than I realized.* The second is, *Sandy and I are off to a rough start.*

"I'm sorry if I insulted you or your car," says Sandy, coming toward him with a hand extended. "It's so nice of you to agree to meet us this morning. And here, no less. We must be inconveniencing you."

KC gives the extended hand a firm shake and says, "I'm very used to my car taking a few hits. My lovely wife, Wanda, always has a lot to say about my car—none of it too flattering for me, I'm afraid. Now, tell me—which of these young soccer stars out here belong to you and Marcel?"

Sandy points out their two boys, lively young players running up and down the field. Watching the boys play, KC thinks of his grandchildren and how important it is that he make time for them. There's something wonderful about watching children play. Their energy, their enthusiasm—it feeds the soul. There's enough action in this soccer game to capture KC's attention. It's not until he hears

Sandy addressing him again that he realizes he's been lost in the game for several minutes.

"I have to say, Kenneth," Sandy says, "that book Marcel brought home for me—I really loved some of the concepts there."

"Oh yeah? What interested you most?"

"Where to start? So many things. I loved the fact that in the United States, once people earn about seventy-five thousand dollars a year, making more money has no impact at all on their day-to-day feelings of happiness. And I loved that bit about how when couples do exciting things together, their relationship itself feels novel and exciting. That's certainly been the case these last few months with Marcel travelling less. We've been able to do a lot more together—exciting things. But I was also really interested in the idea that instead of trying to get more money, we might think about how to use the money we already have to get happier."

Marcel drops an arm around his wife's shoulders and nods along with almost every point she mentions. When she finishes listing off the things that most impressed her about the book, he adds his own two cents. "Something that really resonated with me was the idea that time spent driving is a bust for happiness. But time spent exercising is a boon for happiness. I've been biking to work since I've been at Optimal IT, so I've seen the truth of this firsthand. Taking a bike to work, even occasionally, changed my commute from a grind to a pleasure."

KC can hardly believe how much both Marcel and Sandy have gotten from the book. Seeing this, he's inspired to reread the book himself, this time in tandem with Wanda. After all, they have their own decisions to make and their own issues to discuss.

"One thing that always struck me in that book is how the shift from buying stuff to buying experiences can really affect your happiness," KC says. "Same thing for the shift from spending on yourself to spending on others."

"Oh, for sure!" Sandy says excitedly. "All of the stuff around buying and experience. When I think about the times in our lives when we've been happiest, it's always a family experience. Actually, after we read the book, we sat down and planned a family vacation.

It'll be the first one we've had in years. And just knowing that that's coming up, well, it adds a little splash of happiness to my day every time I think about it."

"Wait—you've already planned a vacation? Does that mean you've firmed up your schedule already? Does that mean you've reached a decision?"

Marcel and Sandy exchange happy smiles. "It does," they say together.

Now it's KC's turn to smile. He can guess the decision they've reached without them having to say it.

"You were right, Ken," Marcel says. "There's more to consider than just dollars. I love the people at Optimal IT. I love what I'm doing there. It's a much better setup for me and for my family. If we have to live with a little less money, so be it. I'm staying. And I'm positive that's the right decision. Because the minute I made it, I felt so energized and, strangely, relaxed at the same time."

The three of them look back out at the soccer field, where one of Marcel and Sandy's sons kicks the ball through the posts for a clean goal. After a chorus of whoops and applause, things settle down, and play resumes.

"Can I ask—what was the real deal maker in your decision?" KC says.

Marcel nods out at the soccer pitch, at his children. "My little soccer champs out there, of course. Staying at Optimal IT means I get to do a lot more of this," he says with an air of calm and a quiet smile.

First thing Monday morning, KC drives over to the Crestwood Inn for another meeting with Karen. These Monday-morning breakfast meetings have become a regular part of their operation. As usual, Karen is already there when he arrives, already deep into her first cup of coffee.

"Good morning, Karen," says KC.

"Don't jump to conclusions, Kenneth. It'll hardly be a good morning if I get bad news on the Marcel front."

KC purses his lips as he debates the ethics of disclosing Marcel's decision to Karen. It's unlikely Marcel will have changed his mind on this point over the last couple of days. KC recalls his cheerful attitude at the soccer pitch. But it's not his place to say anything. This decision is something Marcel ought to tell her himself, so KC decides to keep mum on the matter. Unfortunately, his expression has already betrayed him.

"Okay, Ken. You clearly know something that I don't know. It's written all over your face. So fess up."

"It's just that …"

"It's just that what? Is this a trust issue or something? What are you holding back? From the look on your face, it's not good news."

KC tries to relax his features to keep his face from spilling secrets. "The look on my face has nothing to do with the nature of the news. It's all about confidentiality. And I'm mulling that over. I really shouldn't talk about it. I'm sorry, Karen. It's definitely not a trust issue."

"So you're telling me you know his decision, but you're going to make me sweat it out for another couple of hours?" she says, agitation slowly creeping into her voice.

"I totally understand how you feel. And I can see how much you want to know what happened at my meeting at the soccer pitch. But I also know that you of all people—an HR person—realize that it's not my place to tell you. It's up to Marcel to share his decision with you."

"Wait—what? You met with them at a soccer pitch? What's that about?"

"You're still fishing, Karen. But since you must know, their kids' soccer team won two to zero. And Marcel's oldest boy scored one of those goals."

"All right, all right. I give up," she says, and she slumps back in her chair for a moment. Soon enough, she sits back up and leans across the table, all business again. "Let's talk about the rollout that you're starting with our third department. By the way, I hear you gave some neat advice to Abdul and Jane in your workshop with them. Abdul tried to explain it to me, but I lost him at 'beer commercial.'"

KC laughs, remembering the spiralling beer-commercial conversation he had during that workshop. "Yeah, that turned into a pretty interesting discussion. It all started when Jane asked me if I truly believe that we're often responsible for our own unhappiness."

"And do you?"

"No question about it. Eleanor Roosevelt put this very succinctly when she said, 'No one can make you feel inferior without your consent.'"

"I guess I agree with that."

"Well, Abdul didn't. Just from his body language, it was obvious he wasn't buying any of it. So finally, he said, 'Wait a minute. This is hard for me to believe. I just can't imagine that I would want to do that, to make myself unhappy. How do people make themselves unhappy anyway?' I explained to him that there are hundreds of ways of making yourself unhappy but that they all start the same way: with a sense of craving or rejection. Now, at that point, Rita—"

"I didn't realize this was going to be such a long story," Karen says. "Should I order another latte? If this is going to be one of your epic tales, I'll need a bit more caffeine to see me through it."

Before KC can answer, Karen flags down the server for a refill on her coffee. After the server has topped off her cup and she's taken her first few sips, she looks back at KC.

"Can I continue now?" he asks.

"Please."

"So where was I?"

"Rita. You were about to mention Rita."

KC nods and carries on with the story. He describes how Rita, who was standing next to Abdul during this discussion, declared that she had no trouble with the concept that she makes herself unhappy. "I mean, I do it all the time. I make myself miserable," she said. "This is a real difference between men and women. Isn't it, Ken? This self-awareness."

Looking directly at Karen, KC says, "I thought that was an interesting point. Even today, there are still very big differences between the messages young men typically get in their enculturation and the messages young women typically get. So that's when I told my beer-commercial story."

"Finally! Does this mean we're getting to the point?" Karen asks with obvious impatience. "What's the beer-commercial story?"

"Look, it's a fairly long story, and you already sound a bit agitated."

"For God's sake, Kenneth, just tell me the story already! I'm agitated because I'm unsettled over the Marcel situation, which you refuse to talk about. But I am intrigued to hear this beer-commercial theory—if we could ever actually get to it."

"Okay, here it is."

The gist of KC's theory, as he explains to Karen, is that males often set standards for personal happiness and life satisfaction that they could achieve only if they were to live permanently in a beer commercial—a universe where everyone is good looking and having tons of fun, where life is carefree. Many men will look at a picture of a beautiful woman and feel a sense of desire. But even just that twinge of desire, that craving, creates some unhappiness within them, whether they're aware of it or not. KC speculates that many women will look at exactly the same picture but have a different reaction—a reaction that nonetheless creates at least as much unhappiness for themselves.

KC developed this latter part of the theory a few years ago after a group of professional women asked him to do a presentation on self-esteem in female athletes. Instead, he decided to do a presentation on self-esteem in females as a whole. He went to the local newsstand and asked the clerk to sell him the top 10 women's magazines, the top sellers. Then he asked her for the top 10 men's magazines. However, that turned out to be an impossible request. She didn't have a top 10 for the men—or even a top five—because men don't buy nearly as many magazines as women. His plan was to look at the articles in the women's magazines and see if the central message differed in any meaningful way from the message in the men's magazines. Of course, the messages were totally different. Most of the articles in the women's magazines had tips for how women could improve themselves, an implication that they weren't okay the way they were. But the men's articles were all about ways to save on income taxes or build a better compost box.

In doing this research, he found himself leafing through an issue of *Vanity Fair*. The first 50 pages were mostly just ads featuring attractive female models in beautiful clothes. His longing quotient and, therefore, inner dissatisfaction was subtly increasing page by page. Eventually, he came upon a page on which an incredibly well-built man was strategically holding a pair of underwear in front of his nude body. KC's reaction was to quickly flip the page, but just as he was about to flip this particular page, his wife, who was looking at the magazine over his shoulder, said to him, "Not so fast."

"Really?" he said.

"It's not what you think. I just want you to look at this picture here and compare yourself to this chiselled Adonis."

"Why would I ever do that?"

"That's what women are constantly being asked to do. We're forever comparing ourselves to the impossible beauty standards of models."

KC looks up at Karen and is happy to see she's paying close attention. "In that moment," he says, "I was thankful that I haven't been socialized into believing my self-esteem is based on a comparison to the young man in the picture. And I was particularly thankful for the placement of the model's underwear!" he adds with a light laugh.

Karen rolls her eyes and says, "Move along, please. This is getting embarrassing."

"Look, the point of all of this is simply that we all create unhappiness for ourselves by craving things—even when those things are impossible to achieve. So much of the suffering we go through in our lives is self-created, self-generated. Becoming aware of the push and pull of the cravings and rejections inside of ourselves can help mitigate that."

"And what, may I ask, were Abdul's and Rita's reactions to this theory of yours?"

"Well, Abdul, one of the most practical guys I've ever worked with, immediately wanted to know how long it would take him to divest himself of such thoughts. He wanted a time frame. So I gave him one. I told him he could spend his whole lifetime trying to rid himself of these thoughts and that still probably wouldn't be time enough."

"I'm sure that was very reassuring for him," says Karen, laughing.

"He took it in stride," says KC, joining Karen in bit of laughter.

"You know, Kenneth, I do like certain elements of your theory. There's food for thought there. But let's get back to business. We've got another round of the program to implement this week, and I want to work out some of the particulars."

"Right. On task. Does this mean you're not still agitated about the Marcel situation?"

Karen smiles at him and drains the rest of her coffee. "Of course not. Because I'm pretty sure I've figured out what Marcel told you."

"Really? And what might that be?"

"I'm sorry, Kenneth, but human-resource policy prevents me from telling you—an outside contractor—confidential in-house HR decisions before they're announced to the shareholders."

EPILOGUE

In this section, we learn about how it all turns out and play Golf in the Kingdom.

KC is in the middle of his session with one of the programming groups, when he notices Karen enter the conference room through the back doors and sit down in the back corner. While the programmers split off into smaller groups in which they discuss the merits of energy management versus time management, KC weaves his way through the tables. As he goes, he eavesdrops on the groups and ascertains that as usually happens in these sessions, the programmers are coming to the realization that managing their energy is more valuable and controllable than managing their time.

At the back of the room, he approaches Karen. "What brings you, the HR queen, into our humble midst?"

"I've been promoted to queen, have I?"

"If the royal slipper fits," KC jokes. "So what brings you by?"

"Well, as difficult as it may be for you to believe, I love hearing the info in these sessions. Sometimes it takes a few times for it all to really sink in. I've dipped into a handful of these workshops now, but I'm still finding it hard to actually act like a so-called thermostat day to day. It's a great metaphor, Ken, but it takes constant vigilance to put it into practice."

"Oh, definitely. I mean, I teach this stuff, and I still struggle with it. It's amazing how often I find myself reacting like a thermometer. It's downright embarrassing for me as the so-called expert."

"Well, about that. If I may be so bold, I have an idea that might help us mere mortals keep the thermostat thing at the forefront of our minds."

"Your boldness and mortality are two of the things I like about you, Karen. What are you thinking?"

"The metaphor is great. Everybody who hears it gets it. But implementation is another matter. It needs to be—to use one of your words—operationalized. So here's what I've been doing. I taped a picture of a thermostat, a big one, on the bulletin board in front of my desk as a reminder of how I want to be. Every time I see it, I do a quick check of my energy level and see if it's an appropriate level for the task I'm doing. I also try to notice if any of those energy-draining thoughts or actions are happening. The picture functions as sort of a touchstone."

It's a simple idea, but KC loves it. He's often found that the simplest ideas can be the most effective. "I like it, Karen. It's good. A really good idea."

"Well, that's not the idea. That's just the preamble."

"Oh. Pretty long preamble then. I am in the middle of a workshop here," KC says with a light laugh.

Karen looks at the clustered programmers busily talking among themselves. "Seems like the workshop is running just fine without you at the moment."

"Are you going to tell me the idea or not?"

Karen laughs but relents. "Okay. The idea is to give everyone in each of these sessions a coaster in the shape of a thermostat. And written on the coaster could be some of the key teaching points—you know, reminders of some of the important concepts you've covered in the sessions."

"That's brilliant!"

"Thank you," she says with a satisfied smile.

"And every time one of the participants grabs a cup of coffee or glass of water, they'll be reminded to manage their energy. A constant reminder."

"Just so you know, I did already think of that aspect, Ken. That's why I'm the queen of HR, after all."

"That you are," he says, laughing again—a little too loudly this time, as it turns out. The conversation among the programmers has started to quiet down, and his laughter draws curious looks from the group. "But now, fair queen, I've got to get back to the group here. Can we meet for lunch?"

"I'm sure there must be more-formal protocol around asking a queen to lunch," she says, adopting a dramatic and queenly air about her. "But nonetheless, I'll accept your invitation, oh noble subject."

Karen dominates the lunchtime conversation as she shares story after story about the many ways in which energy management applications have been spreading throughout the company.

"People are really starting to think in terms of energy management," she says. "They're focused on energy, not just time. I walked by a meeting room the other day and heard Amy, who was leading the session, say, 'Time is tight, but let's not get caught up in that. In our last ten minutes here, we're going to act like we have time. We'll get more done, and we won't drown in anxiety.' And it worked! They got a ton done."

"That's great to hear!"

"I also ran into Brian last week. He told me he's found the perfect opportunity to practice his meditative breathing at the office."

"Oh yeah? When's that?"

"While waiting for Microsoft Office to update!" She describes how these updates used to drive Brian crazy; he used to just sit in front of his computer screen, trying to will the download stripe to move quicker. By the time Brian actually got to use the computer, he was already fuming. But now he sits back and focuses on his breathing while his computer is busy updating itself. The longer these updates take, the more relaxed he gets.

"Ha! I like it," says KC.

"Oh, and let's not forget about all our outdoor space. Yesterday Douglas and I had a meeting out by the picnic tables. We're trying to promote that sort of thing. I mean, our office is in such a beautiful setting. Why not take advantage of it?"

"This is music to my ears, Karen."

Karen smiles and carries on. She explains that Douglas has decided to purchase sleeping pods for the office, and he's redesigning some on-site spaces to serve as mini rest-and-recovery areas. "We want people to have more flexibility in their working hours. We're even getting everyone sleep-monitoring devices as part of their overall profit-sharing plan. That last one was Douglas's idea."

"Sounds like Douglas has really hopped on board."

"He absolutely has. And speaking of him, he asked me to tell you that he wants to meet with you first thing Monday morning. You available?"

"Well, sure, I think so."

"But he did tell me to warn you—the meeting will take at least five hours."

"Five hours! I'm not sure I have that kind of time. What the heck does he want to talk about for five hours anyway?"

From the sly smile on Karen's face, KC can see he's somehow been had, but he's not sure what she's getting at. *Five hours? What kind of meeting lasts five hours?* Then it dawns on him. "Ah, golf game!" he cries.

"That's it, Ken. You're to meet him on the first tee at the Shivas Irons Country Club at eight o'clock. He says to bring you're a game. According to him, that centring breathing technique of yours has him playing near-scratch golf."

"Shivas Irons? That's supposed to be a sensational course. I know he'll have a huge advantage on me, but honestly, I'll be happy just to play that course!"

"I don't want to hear that kind of talk, Ken. I've got ten dollars on you. I promised Douglas you'd bring him down a notch."

On his way to the parking lot, while daydreaming about the upcoming golf game, KC gets a call from Bill at the radio station, who wants to cue up their next show. They do a bit of work, outlining the content for their upcoming show, and once they've finished, Bill asks, "Have you ever heard of a psychologist named Don Greene?"

"Hmm, the name sounds familiar. Is he the guy who works with musicians at Juilliard?"

"One and the same. I saw a short clip of him on YouTube the other day. I think you'd like him. He wasn't speaking specifically about energy management, but everything he presented seemed to apply to it. I especially liked this part where he said that the voice in your head is not God. So you should be free to tell it to shut up!"

Alone in the parking lot, KC lets out a big laugh. He says, "I can see why you'd like that one, Bill."

"He was working with an organist who had a lot of jaw tension, especially when he made a mistake. Greene gave him three steps to follow. One, accept the mistake. Two, unclench the jaw. Three, cue yourself with certain words or a piece of music. It made me think of that time you told me about teaching golf pros on the tour to hum, whistle or sing quietly to themselves whenever they felt pressure. You said that sort of thing could help them get back into the flow of their swing."

"It's a similar technique. Both are good. Especially for people who get caught up judging their performance while they're performing. That sort of thinking can really throw your energy off course."

"That's exactly what always happens to me when I golf—constant judgment."

"As it happens, I'll actually be golfing next week. So I'll get the chance to put both of these techniques into practice."

"Golfing, huh? Where are you playing?"

"Shivas Irons."

Bill lets out an appreciative whistle. "I played that course once. Oh, now, that's a fantastic course."

"You got any advice then? To be honest, I'm a little nervous to be playing such a fine course. And I've got some pretty stiff competition."

"Advice? Sure. Get the ball in the hole."

"Thanks, Bill. Sage words, as always," KC says.

"Actually, I do have a bit of real advice. It's something I heard Hugh Downs say when he was talking about how he dealt with nerves as a young broadcaster. He said to concentrate on *what* you're doing, not *how* you're doing it."

"Sound advice from a veteran broadcaster."

"See you soon, Ken."

On a bright, sunny Monday morning, KC pulls into the country club in his beautiful MGB. He knows this is as good as he'll look all day.

"Morning, hotshot," Douglas says, wandering out from the pro shop. "What a glorious morning for a game of golf, huh?"

"Thanks for the invitation, Douglas. Were your usual victims out of town? Did you need a new sacrificial lamb?"

"I never choose a golf partner based on ability. I've found that long after you've forgotten someone's score, you remember their behaviour and whether or not they're fun to be with. So I have a feeling we're going to have a great morning!"

They tee off, getting a great game started. KC plays pretty well through the first half of the course. He's no pro golfer, but he does a good job of managing his energy, and he's able to hold his own.

Somewhere on the back nine, as KC is—amazingly—about to putt for par, Douglas once again confesses his initial skepticism about the energy management program.

"But I'm astounded at the change, Ken. And it's been such a simple intervention, really. In retrospect, I can see why the program worked so well. We focus on energy management in every aspect of organizational life, except with our employees—with the people who actually do the work. I mean, we go to great lengths to make our machines faster, our buildings more efficient and our technology more productive. It should be obvious that our people need an energy management system upgrade too." He pauses to shake his head. "It's so blindingly obvious. I just can't believe we didn't see it earlier."

KC smiles and steps up to his ball. Setting his putter in place, he begins to hum to himself, a calming little tune that helps him relax his stance—and his mind. KC taps the ball gently, just as he intended, and watches it roll over the green, straight into the hole.

THE LAST WORD

In this section, the author, Peter Jensen, summarizes key energy management concepts introduced by Kenneth Coghill in the preceding novel.

In the introduction to this book, I presented the metaphor of the thermostat versus the thermometer and outlined the benefits to performance and health that come from setting the temperature rather than rising and falling to reflect the environment. With this metaphor as a foundation, the novel focused on the skills and behaviours required to do one of three things:

1. Turn the thermostat down (i.e., lower our energy levels)
2. Turn the thermostat up (i.e., raise our energy levels)
3. Minimize energy leaks (i.e., ensure that we have enough fuel for the thermostat in the first place)

To make the concepts crystal clear, I summarize these skill sets below.

TURNING THE THERMOSTAT DOWN: THE LINK BETWEEN HIGH AROUSAL AND PERFORMANCE ERRORS

Why do we sometimes need to turn down the thermostat? High arousal (the technical term for energy) leads to a narrow attentional focus. Intuitively, we know this. When someone is upset or angry, we'll often make the decision not to talk to that person, because we know he or she won't be able to take in what we're trying to tell him or her. In sports, a high energy, or arousal, level can quickly lead to the most-dreaded fate: choking. The narrow attentional focus brought on by high arousal makes it easy to miss relevant cues necessary for performance. I'm using some jargon here, I know, so let me put all of this information into plain English by way of an example.

You go into a meeting with a proposal you hope people will respond well to. Yesterday you spoke to Monica, one of the key decision makers, who made it clear she was on board with your idea. But now, when you've barely started your presentation, Monica interrupts to say, "I really don't see why we're considering this. It doesn't fit with any of our other ideas. Frankly, we could better spend our time in this meeting by discussing something else."

What impact will Monica's statement have on you in that meeting? Well, let's look at it on different levels. In the novel, Kenneth introduced the skill of active awareness, which is about being aware of what's happening inside you on the mind, body and feelings levels. He explained that we are not our minds, bodies or feelings. Because we have a self, a point of observation, we can become aware of what's going on at each of these three levels without letting them control us.

Let's apply this concept to the Monica situation. What will you experience at these levels as a result of her abrupt change in attitude toward your proposal? At the body level, your face might redden, you might cross your arms, your heart rate might elevate and your palms might sweat. At the feelings level, you might feel frustrated, anxious, nervous, angry, or any combination of those. What might you say to yourself? Your mind might start panicking, giving you all sorts of messages at once. *I thought she was on board with the idea! I can't believe she would do this to me! What am I going to say? I've got to pull this together.*

All of these thoughts, feelings and physical reactions seem to be happening at once, overwhelming you. You don't know how to respond, so you leave the meeting thoroughly dissatisfied. However, 10 minutes later, back in your office, you're suddenly able to think of all of the things you wish you'd said and done. *I should have said this. I should have said that. And I didn't even think of this, this or this.*

Why couldn't you access that information while you were in front of Monica in the meeting? Because you became what was happening to you. What was going on at the mind, body and feelings levels dominated you. You were not in control; your mind, body and feelings were. Your arousal spiked, your attentional focus narrowed and you couldn't access critical information. You choked.

In short, if we are to avoid choking, we need to learn how to turn the thermostat down.

KEY SKILL FOR TURNING THE THERMOSTAT DOWN: CENTRING
The most powerful tool at your disposal for turning the thermostat down is breathing—in particular, centring.

The centring breathing exercise that Kenneth introduced to the basketball team stops the inner noise in its tracks and redirects our attention elsewhere—to our breath. On the inhalation, we bring 100 percent of our attention to the diaphragm, and on the exhalation, we bring our attention to our shoulders, which drop, and our knees, which bend.

Centring is an exceptional skill that comes from aikido. It's practical and unobtrusive, so you can do it anywhere. No one will even know you're doing it, because frankly, people expect you to breathe. It's also easy to find opportunities to practice centring. You can do it while sitting at your desk, waiting in line at a supermarket checkout, or sitting in a mile-long traffic jam.

Being stuck in a traffic jam is actually one of the best moments to practice centring, because when you're stuck in traffic, you only have two choices: learn to fly or learn to breathe. In this situation, you wouldn't put your car into neutral and push the gas pedal to the floor, because doing so would be a waste of fuel and energy, would be hard on the car's engine and wouldn't get you anywhere anyway. It would be a useless action. Often, however, in this same situation, we push our internal gas pedal to the floor, wasting energy and damaging an engine that's much more valuable than the car's. It's an equally useless action.

There is a complete description of centring in chapter 6, wherein KC is teaching the concept to the basketball players, and I've also included a detailed set of instructions on centring at the end of this short chapter. For now, though, it's important to realize that awareness is the key here. Once you become aware of something, you have a chance to change it. However, as long as you're unaware, you will remain unconsciously incompetent. Often, noticing an issue is all it takes to effect some change.

Stop reading for a minute. Close your eyes, go inside and notice your jaw muscles. Notice any tension you have in your forehead. Take a few seconds to do that.

What did you do when you noticed tension? That's right—you simply let go. You didn't have to learn anything. You just needed to be aware that the tension was there so that you could do something about it. We would do well to check in with ourselves at various points in our day and simply make small adjustments that allow us to conserve energy, put ourselves in a better mindset and keep problems from escalating. On the day of a big competition, meeting or presentation, monitoring our arousal levels is a great way to conserve the energy we need in order to perform our best.

Athletes often ask me, "How often should I centre?" My answer to them is the same as to anyone: "Centre as often as needed."

Beyond centring, I outline some additional skills people can use to reduce energy levels in the section that follows, which focuses on minimizing the drain.

TURNING THE THERMOSTAT UP: THE CASE FOR TURNING UP

Let's take a look at what can happen when our arousal level is too low. When arousal is low, our attentional focus becomes broad, and we start making errors of overinclusion—we get bored and distracted, daydreaming and paying attention to everything but what we need to do: our work. We can't seem to find the energy or focus to work well. We become inefficient and distracted. For example, while in a meeting, you might suddenly look up and realize that you have no idea what's been going on for the past 15 minutes.

We call this phenomenon the flat syndrome. It tends to hit most of us in the early to midafternoon. In those moments, you feel tired, unmotivated and maybe a little bit negative.

This state of being affects our ability to think. Glucose, which is the primary source of energy for the body's cells, including brain cells, becomes depleted when you continuously exert effort on a difficult thinking and reasoning task. When what you are doing requires a heavy dose of working memory—which most cognitive tasks do—you need to supply energy for the brain. Rather than running full steam ahead, you will be far more productive if you take a step back and reenergize. If you don't take time to recoup your resources, your performance can suffer. Operating with all glucose cylinders on empty is a worse option, especially for those people who have the most cognitive horsepower and potential to begin with.

Turning the thermostat up can be about acquiring energy. The first important fundamental here is sleep. You might recall that in chapter 11, Ken and Bill did an entire radio show on sleep, naps and the importance of rest and recovery.

Raising your thermostat can also be about sharpening the saw. You might also recall KC talking to the synchronized swimmer about energizing in order to be able to deal with the difficult practices she and her teammates were going through. Chapter 8 focuses entirely on energizing. KC encourages the synchronized swimmer to act abnormally in order to supply energy to herself and her teammates. This type of energizing is all about choosing to turn your thermostat up when the situation needs energy but the task is close to the last thing you feel like doing.

SKILLS FOR TURNING THE THERMOSTAT UP
1. Take breaks.
You'll recall a moment in the novel when Kenneth encourages one radio listener to take smoke breaks. Kenneth isn't advocating

smoking, of course, but the idea of building regular breaks into your day. Smokers seem to have no trouble finding time to take a break every 90 minutes. Non-smokers should be able to do the same. Getting deliberate about taking breaks, especially if those breaks can take us outdoors, is a primary way of ensuring we have the energy we need to perform throughout our busy days. Breaks can help turn up the thermostat.

2. Focus on purpose and meaning.

Having a sense of purpose and meaning can be another great source of energy. It's difficult to be motivated when we feel as if we're being pushed and shoved by circumstances—by what's happening moment after moment, hour after hour, throughout the day. A vision or purpose gives us a sense of direction and keeps us on course. Airplane pilots have told me that in turbulent weather, the plane is often pushed off course. Every time this happens, however, the autopilot rectifies things and gets the plane back on track. It's too bad we don't come with an autopilot preinstalled! We need to create our own autopilot, and a vision can fulfill this function. A clear and compelling mental image of the future, of where we're going, helps keep us on course.

Part of having a purpose and meaning is to help make sense of what's important to us in our lives and what we are doing. The noble cause the Canadian women's hockey team used in the Sochi Olympics is one such example. In the second to last chapter of the book, Marcel and his wife, Sandra, discover that when you look at all of the assets in a situation—in their case, they originally neglected to look at personal happiness—the right decision to make becomes much more obvious.

3. Humour equals energy.

A timely quip or someone bringing lightness into a difficult moment is often greatly appreciated and energizing. I attempted to write this book in a manner that was lighthearted and energizing in order to make it an easy read. I believe that I often learned more in a pub than I did in a classroom. Humour is the grease of life.

MINIMIZING THE DRAIN: WHY IS IT IMPORTANT?

When we talk about energy levels, we have to consider the effect of proper nutrition and exercise. Many great books have been written on the importance of these two factors on our overall health and energy. But it's also important to consider all of the ways in which we deplete energy resources. Self-defeating thinking, for example, is a huge waste of energy, and the associated negative impact this kind of thinking has on our self-esteem and confidence levels only amplifies the energy drain. Even if we're eating the right foods and getting lots of exercise, a few self-defeating thoughts can destroy our energy level. Therefore, we need to learn to minimize all of the drains on our energy resources. In my workshops, I often use the metaphor of a home-energy audit (you might remember Kenneth using this same technique with Dominic). It's easy for workshop participants to identify energy drains from their homes: leaving the lights on in a room, standing in front of the fridge with the door wide open, having poorly insulated windows—it's a list that could go on and on. I ask participants to think about these home-related energy losses as a metaphor for the mental aspect of energy.

Think of it this way. When you leave a room, ideally, you turn out the lights. Then, as you enter a new room, you flip on a new set of lights. Similarly, when I finish working on one aspect of an assignment, I imagine turning out the lights, which are metaphorically equivalent to my attentional focus, on that project. After a brief break, I'm ready to get back to work, so I imagine walking into another room and turning on another set of the lights, focusing my attention on that project. I don't want to be draining my energy by shifting focus constantly between the two projects. I want to be focused on what I'm doing at the time.

SKILLS FOR MINIMIZING THE DRAIN

1. Changing Positions or Moving

This tip is fairly self-explanatory. It ties in with the need to take breaks. Move around, do some stretches, take those breaks and get outside if you can.

2. Ceaseless Striving

Most of us are pretty good at applying effort to situations in which we know we can make a difference. We tend to stumble, however, when we insist on applying this same kind of effort to situations that are unchangeable and unfixable. Trying to change the unchangeable is an enormous energy waster. Imagine if I asked you to change what you had for breakfast this morning. Ridiculous! But that's essentially what our efforts to change unchangeable situations amount to. The key skill here is learning to let go.

Let me tell you a story that illustrates this point. Several years ago, I had a meeting at seven o'clock in the evening with the medical and scientific committee of a sport's governing body. A few minutes before the meeting, the chairman, who knew me well, said to me, "You're not your usual chipper self this evening, Jensen."

"Bah, of course I am," I said.

The chairman shrugged and said, "Suit yourself. But from my vantage point, I don't see your usual energy and enthusiasm."

I went inside to check things out for myself and discovered that the chairman was right. I was irritated. I was a little off. Retracing the day in my mind, I realized that I'd been full of energy at lunchtime, but by dinner, frankly, I'd been a lousy company for my family. I reviewed what had happened between lunch and dinner and remembered that I'd gotten a phone call at three o'clock from an individual I didn't have much respect for. He'd asked me to do something—something I thought was unethical—and had promised me no money for doing it. The phone call had happened four hours earlier, but there I was, still letting it have an impact on me. I was giving this person way too much attention and influence over me. I decided I had to just let him go.

Now when I have to let something go, I try to find a suitable metaphor for the thing in question so that I can visualize it clearly. I shan't tell you what this particular individual reminded me of, but you might get the picture when I tell you that in my imagination, I flushed him down the toilet. And when I say I flushed him down the toilet, I mean in full detail. There he was, swirling in the bowl, his tie out in Dilbert position, his pompous voice wailing, "You can't do this to me!" Then he was gone, with nothing but a slight film left on the water. Detail is important!

Letting go is a vital skill in life. We have to be able to decide what we have control over and what we don't have control over. If you don't learn to make this distinction, you're in for a long, hard life. You're in for a lifetime of massive drains on your energy resources.

Karen at first won't even consider apologizing to her sister (i.e., letting go) in chapter 10, but when she finally does, the relief of getting rid of the rock in her shoe is palpable.

3. Negative Thinking

You're thinking negatively when you fear the future, put yourself down, criticize yourself excessively for small errors, doubt your ability and expect failure. The internalized critic has no value, yet it's often incredibly persuasive—and an energy drainer.

You're thinking positively, and realistically, when you recognize all of who you are—which is a good deal more than just your limitations. You're also thinking positively when you challenge the critic.

Negative thoughts have a tendency to flit into and out of our consciousness without us noticing their significance. However, our failure to notice the significance of these thoughts doesn't stop them from doing damage. Challenge your negative thinking, and learn to remember all of who you are.

4. Overwhelming Self

In the same way that a single important event—such as making a speech, for example—can throw our arousal level up and cause us to miss critical information, so can a day-to-day diet of overwhelming messages. These messages are the stories we tell ourselves—how much time we have, how important something is, what other people will think of us, etc. The list is endless.

At one point in the novel, Kenneth outlines the sequence of events that lead Dominic to overwhelm himself in his relationship with Henri. Kenneth explains this sequence in terms of layers.

The first layer consists of the stories we tell ourselves. The second layer consists of the images that come from the parts of the story that we start to imagine. Images act as events on the body. Once we start imagining things, corresponding feelings and emotions arise. This brings us to the third layer: feelings. Our feelings and emotions elevate our arousal level. Maintaining a heightened arousal level over the long term is bad news for our performance and our general well-being. Kenneth's advice to Dominic is to redirect the energy that each emotion brings about toward more-productive behaviour. For example, if you're angry, you could put the energy that anger brings about to productive use by vacuuming the house or scrubbing the shower.

One way we often overwhelm ourselves is by focusing on end goals rather than performance goals. It's easy to become overwhelmed when we get caught up in the all of what we have to achieve instead of focusing on one step at a time. Sometimes we forget to notice the satisfaction that comes from completing each individual step of a larger project. It's a terrible shame to neglect to notice these little satisfactions, because they can lead to increased confidence and self-esteem.

Here's a simple equation I like to use to remember this point:

Breaking Up Big Tasks = Sense of Achievement

What we imagine is also important. I spoke above about the power of having a positive vision. Strong, clear imagery can help pull you toward your goal. Imagery can, however, also steer you the other way. When you imagine things that aren't beneficial to your performance, you're pushing yourself away from your goal. Imagining that you don't have enough time is a perfect example of negative imagery.

Kenneth offers some simple advice to combat this issue of time. When you feel pressed for time, try acting as if you have all the time in the world. You'll be surprised how much this opens up your sense of time and lightens your load. By acting as if you have time, you lower your arousal level, which broadens your attentional focus and allows you to work more efficiently and quickly on the task at hand. It's one of the paradoxes of life: when you slow down, you actually acquire time and finish what you're doing more quickly.

5. Multitasking

My advice on multitasking is this: don't do it. Focus on one thing at a time, and do that thing. Don't continuously interrupt yourself to answer e-mails or phone calls. Get rid of everything that diffuses your attention and drains your energy. Focusing on a single task is far more efficient and productive than multitasking, and it will help you maintain your energy longer.

In chapter 7, Kenneth helps the group at Optimal IT move away from a diffuse multitasking focus and come up with a single focus plan. This is not dissimilar to his session with Farhan in chapter 9, when KC asks him to pick just one member of his staff to focus his attentions on—someone who will appreciate his time and effort. That way, the chances for success are high and energizing.

6. Awful-izing

This concept is tied to number two, learning to let go. Ben Zandler, the conductor of the Boston Philharmonic Orchestra, talks about the "conversation of no possibilities." Everyone knows this conversation. It's the one where we talk about how bad things are, how unfair it all is, how nothing will make it better and on and on. It's this kind of conversation that Kenneth first encounters when he visits Optimal IT. This conversation of no possibilities can pull us closer to other people, but it doesn't take us anywhere. It's easy to get stuck in this conversation, so it's important to have a skill that can get us out of it. That skill is reframing.

Reframing is about recognizing that although life might choose the information, you choose the perspective you take on that information. I once worked with a company that was going through a second major change in the course of four or five months. Many people were complaining bitterly about the change even though they recognized that it had to be made. We talked about how difficult it had been to go through the first change, and the thought of having to go through a second one had the whole team down in the dumps.

"How do you want to handle this?" I asked. "Do you really want to go through this with the same negative energy as the last time?"

My point was that they couldn't do anything about the fact that the change was going to happen, but they could decide how they would face it. They could choose to have a better, more-energy-efficient perspective on the situation than they'd had the first time around.

7. Changing Your Perception of Stress

Dr. Kelly McGonigal, a Stanford University health psychologist, is on a mission to make people happier and healthier. For years, she instructed her patients on methods of avoiding stress. But now she's speaking out about how recent research suggests that she's been giving the wrong advice all along. Her new philosophy is this: "The old understanding of stress as an unhelpful relic of our animal instincts is being replaced by the understanding that stress actually makes us socially smart—it's what allows us to be fully human."

The problem is that we view signs of stress (e.g., increased heart rate, sudden sweating, etc.) as signs of anxiety. Change your mindset to view these physiological effects as signs that your body is preparing itself to meet the challenge ahead. Viewing stress symptoms as helpful prevents your blood vessels from constricting (the stress-induced contraction of blood vessels is one of the reasons chronic stress is typically related to cardiovascular disease). When you adopt the mindset that stress is helpful, your blood vessels actually look similar to the way they look in moments of joy or courage.

DETAILED CENTRING INSTRUCTIONS

You can perform this skill while standing or sitting. If you're sitting, make sure you're upright so that your diaphragm is open and free to receive air.

Focus your attention on the path of your breath. Inhale slowly and deeply through your nose, allowing the air to travel down into your diaphragm (which is located right under the centre of your rib cage, just above your stomach). As your diaphragm fills with air, you will feel it rise. As you exhale, you will feel it fall. When you are first learning this skill, it's helpful to sit in a chair, tip your pelvis forward into a bit of a slouch and place your hand on your diaphragm so that you can feel and see the rise and fall of your body. This awareness gives you a feedback check on whether or not you're breathing all the way down into your diaphragm.

Once you have taken a complete breath, pause for a second. Then slowly let the air out through your mouth. Allow the air to take twice as long to leave your body as it took to breathe it in. As the breath leaves your body, check your jaw for tension and loosen it. Let your shoulders drop and relax. If you're sitting, relax into your buttocks, and let yourself sink into the chair. If you're standing, let your knees soften.

Repeat this process in a focused way as many times as you need to. Even two to three deep breaths will relax your entire mind-and-body system.

IN SUMMARY

1. Breathe in through your nose.
2. Focus 100 percent of your attention on your diaphragm as it fills with air.
3. Pause.
4. Slowly let the breath out through your mouth.
5. As you breathe out, shift your attention to your jaw, which loosens; your shoulders, which drop; and your knees, which soften, or your buttocks, which sink.
6. Repeat as needed.

REFERENCES

Beilock, Sian. *Choke*. Carlton, Vic.: Melbourne UP, 2011.

Benson, Herbert. *The Relaxation Response*. New York: Morrow, 1975.

Borysenko, Joan, and Larry Rothstein. *Minding the Body, Mending the Mind*. Reading, MA: Addison-Wesley Pub., 1987.

Cabane, Olivia Fox. *The Charisma Myth: How Anyone Can Master the Art and Science of Personal Magnetism*. New York: Portfolio/Penguin, 2012.

Castaneda, Carlos. *The Teachings of Don Juan: A Yaqui Way of Knowledge*. New York: Simon and Schuster, 1968.

Dunn, Elizabeth, and Michael I. Norton. *Happy Money: The Science of Smarter Spending*. New York: Simon and Schuster, 2013.

Gellman, Lindsay, and Shayndi Raice. "Banks Reassess Internship Programs, Relax Rules for Junior Employees." *Wall Street Journal*. January 11, 2014.

Heath, Chip, and Dan Heath. *Switch: How to Change Things When Change Is Hard*. New York: Broadway, 2010.

Kotter, John P., and Dan S. Cohen. *The Heart of Change: Real-Life Stories of How People Change Their Organizations*. Boston, MA: Harvard Business School, 2002.

Loehr, Jim, and Tony Schwartz. *The Power of Full Engagement: Managing Energy, Not Time, Is the Key to High Performance and Positive Renewal*. Crows Nest, NSW: Allen and Unwin, 2003.

Logan, David, John Paul King, and Halee Fischer-Wright. *Tribal Leadership: Leveraging Natural Groups to Build a Thriving Organization*. New York: Collins, 2008.

McGonigal, Kelly. *The Upside of Stress: Why Stress Is Good for You, and How to Get Good at It*. N.p.: Avery Pub Group, 2015.

Napier, Nancy K. "The Myth of Multitasking: Think You Can Multitask Well? Think Again." *Psychology Today*. May 12, 2014, https://www.psychologytoday.com/blog/creativity-without-borders/201405/the-myth-multitasking.

Seligman, Martin E. P. *Authentic Happiness: Using the New Positive Psychology to Realize Your Potential for Lasting Fulfillment*. New York: Free, 2002.

Seligman, Martin E. P. *Learned Optimism*. New York: AA Knopf, 1991.

Whitmore, John. *Coaching for High Performance*, 4th Edition. N.p.: Nicholas Brealey Publishing, 2009.

Zander, Rosamund Stone, and Benjamin Zander. *The Art of Possibility*. Boston, MA: Harvard Business School, 2000.

Zukav, Gary. *The Seat of the Soul*. New York: Fireside, 1990.

ABOUT THE AUTHOR

Peter Jensen, PhD has worked with high performers in sport and business for over 40 years. He has attended eight Olympic Games as a member of the Canadian team, and helped over 70 Canadian athletes medal. He teaches at the Queen's School of Business, and is the author of *The Inside Edge* and *Ignite the Third Factor*. Jensen lives in Toronto, Canada.

Printed in the United States
By Bookmasters